my body, the buddhist

my body, the buddhist

DEBORAH HAY

with a foreword by Susan Foster

WESLEYAN UNIVERSITY PRESS

Published by University Press of New England

Hanover & London

WESLEYAN UNIVERSITY PRESS

Published by University Press of New England,

Hanover, NH 03755

© 2000 by Deborah Hay

Printed in the United States of America

5 4 3 2 1

Chapter 8 first appeared in *Contact Quarterly* 22, no. 1
(winter/spring 1997), and again in *PAJ*, a journal of
performance and art, 21, no. 3 (September 1999).
Chapter 15 appeared in *Artlies* 18 (1998), published
in Houston, Texas.

Library of Congress Cataloging-in-Publication Data
Hay, Deborah.

My body, the Buddhist / Deborah Hay.

  p. cm.

ISBN 0-8195-6436-2 (cloth : alk. paper) —

ISBN 0-8195-6328-5 (pb. : alk. paper)

1. Modern dance. 2. Body, Human (Phihosophy)

3. Choreography. I. Title.

GV1783 .H37 2000

792.8'2—dc21   00-008647

Frontispiece: Deborah Hay in *Voilà*. Photo © 1997
by Phyllis Liedecker

dedicated to dance audiences in the 21st century

contents

a chronicle of performance practices by Deborah Hay, 103

To read about a specific dance:

the six dances described in the book and the chapters
containing material about them are listed below.

foreword   *Susan Leigh Foster*

Introducing Deborah Hay's body-as-Buddhist. Such an agile body, capable of lightning-quick transformations—floppy then precise, always deft, full of buffoonery and deadly serious in its commitment to each gesture. It gallops, swaggers, tip-toes, and falls gently backward into the embrace of space. Scrambling or gliding to standing, it grimaces. The softest leaps, the most preposterous gestures, it happily cavorts before slowing to stillness, a dynamic tranquillity. The flexibility, the unpredictability of its attitudes draw us toward it. It gazes back at those who view it with a generous invitation to be looked at.

This body, it is proposed, practices a religion renowned for its skeptical stance toward religion. It performs as teacher, oracle, and companion in the investigation, not of spirituality, but of consciousness itself. Alternately a corporeal provocateur that poses the question of consciousness and the medium through which the investigation of consciousness takes shape, the Buddhist body moves matter-of-factly through its day.

Hay has cultivated this body, discovered and rediscovered it over many years of dancing. In training to make and perform dances, she attends to the body's changeability. She explores the ramifications of multiple, distinctive metaphorical framings of physicality. Body, in turn, has offered a kind of dialogue—probing, assessing, reacting, and instigating—in response to Hay's various queries. Close and consistent attentiveness to this dialogue forms the basis of Hay's regimen for learning to dance and also generates the motional matter from which her dances are made. For Hay, choreography emerges from her ongoing reflections about bodiliness.

My Body, The Buddhist documents this generative play between corporeality and consciousness and between the dance of everyday life and dance as a theatrical practice. The text's non-narrative account of a choreographer's daily work mingles descriptions of living, training, creating, and performing so as to illuminate the integral relation between artistic vision and the daily pursuit of that vision. Fleshing out the body's "daringly ordinary perspicacity," she sustains the quizzical, illusive maverickness of body even as she illumines corporeal existence through her descriptions of it.

ALTERNATIVE ARTISTRY

As a dancer with the Merce Cunningham Dance Company, a participant in the Judson Dance Theater performances, an independent choreographer located in Austin, Texas, and as world-touring performer and teacher, Hay has elaborated a powerful alternative dancing practice. She is continuously upheaving our assumptions about dance and the body. She shows us how interesting stillness is, and how quickly physical commitment can change from one action, persona, or image to another. Her dances elaborate a theatricality that appears pedestrian, intimate, and casual one minute while filled with wonderment, alterity, and sumptuousness the next. Above all, her work invites us to laugh at our own seriousness and take in the dancing seriously, both at the same time. Hay's sustained dedication to alternative choreographic values such as these is an extraordinary achievement, especially during this era of lack of support, monetary and otherwise, for the arts.

During the 1960s, when Hay came of age as an artist, art-making was one of several alternative cultural practices through which mainstream values were critically interrogated. Works by Cunningham, Paul Taylor, Eleo Pomare, and the Judson choreographers all pushed at the boundaries of acceptable dance movement and introduced alternative vocabularies and stagings for danced performance. One of the results of their efforts has been to make evident the specificity of the relationship between technical competence and choreographic vision. Unlike ballet, where standard criteria of evaluation and a universalist ideal of expertise are developed, Hay and others of her generation have proposed projects that require radically alternative sets of physical skills. Unlike modern dance pioneers such as Martha Graham and Doris Humphrey, whose vocabularies seemed to issue from pan-human psychic dynamics, choreographers from the 1960s shifted the focus away from psychological origins and toward the physical matter of dance-making. Their work demonstrates how each new choreographic project requires special skills and hence special training in order for the dancer to acquire those skills.

Hay's work exemplifies a radical and fully realized vision of this kind of alternative training program and choreography. Many contemporary choreographers blur or obscure the ways that training inculcates aesthetic values by working with pick-up companies whose dancers acquire an amalgamation of dance styles, such as release work, contact improvisation, and ballet. Hay, instead, nurtures the relationship between her approach to dance training and performance, and she stands by its integrity. As a result, her dances look entirely unique and so do the dancers who perform them.

Hay has pursued her alternative artistic practice as both choreographer and teacher. From 1980 to 1995 Hay conducted a series of large group workshops in Austin, Texas, each meeting daily for a period of three to four months and culminating in performances of an evening-length work developed over the course of the workshop. Here again, Hay's commitment to the intrinsic connection between learning dancing and making dances is evident. Hay organized each workshop around the exploration of a specific theme, and then allowed the dance to develop from the daily practice of this theme. Rather than instruct students in a standard repertoire of technical skills and then proceed to fashion a dance, Hay organizes both the acquisition of technique and the choreography around a focused inquiry into bodiliness.

Hay's workshops have made the most brilliant dancers better dancers, but they have had equal relevance for people in other professions. Architects, therapists, writers, and construction workers have all participated in these annual gatherings. Here a heterogeneous alternative group of individuals gains bodily eloquence, perceptual acuity, and collective sensibilities that enrich the Austin community and the international dance world. The workshops carry forward the 1960s impulse to include all bodies in dancing, to claim that all bodies can dance, yet they deepen that impulse by requiring such a powerful commitment to the process of physical inquiry.

Hay's alternative artistry has challenged general assumptions about what dance is, and she has also turned its critical reflexivity toward her own artistic practice. *My Body, The Buddhist* witnesses Hay's willingness to examine the limits of her own artistic practice. In one instance, she recounts her abhorrence at the thought of making a dance to a specific piece of music, her sudden awareness of the strict limits this has placed on her own choreography, and her reluctant resolve to embark on the project. Rarely do we glimpse the role of this kind of instrospective reflection in the process of art-making. Hay's staging of the dialogue between body and consciousness generously allows us to view it from many perspectives.

My Body, The Buddhist describes the development of several recent works, focusing especially on how the dances issue from Hay's daily dialogue with body. Hay's previous book, *Lamb at the Altar: The Story of a Dance*, documents the process of creating and producing a single evening-length work developed during one of her large group workshops. In it Hay recounts her responses to the distinctive physicalities of individual participants and the staging of those bodies as characters and actions. Alongside this discussion of bodies and movement, she reports the negotiations concerning a performance space, costuming, scenery, and lighting that are entailed in the mounting of any production. The juxtaposition of these different aspects of dance-making provides an invaluable perspective on how an artist lives and works in these times. *My Body, The Buddhist* continues this chronicle of an artist's work, yet it looks more introspectively at the relationship between a choreographer's daily movement practice and choreographed performance, and it illuminates the dancer's constant and daily attentiveness to body's articulateness.

"WHERE I AM IS WHAT I NEED, CELLULARLY"

One of the dominant and sustaining metaphors in Hay's cultivation of physicality is her postulation of body as the ever-changing cumulative performance of seventy-five trillion semi-independent cells.* In her daily training, Hay practices sensitizing herself to the

---

*Hay recently revised the figure up from fifty-three trillion cells, in keeping with the latest scientific tallies on the body's cell count. She reminisces: "When I began this practice in 1970 I was using the image of 5 million cells. That is how time has changed the body!!" Personal communication.

mobility and responsiveness of body as so constituted. For example, she may use as focus for herself and her students such statements as "Where I am is what I need, cellularly," or "Alignment is everywhere," or "What if Now is Here is Harmony." Such instructions cultivate the differentiatedness of body—the many distinctive possibilities for physical articulation—and the attentiveness required to track and take note of the body's inclinations. They also challenge the dancer to open up to an immense range of neuromuscular possibilities and to validate each of these new impulses. Any and all cellular initiatives are worthy of attention. They are all what the dancer "needs."

In her daily practice of dancing and in the classes she teaches, Hay's use of these directives summons the dancer into the creative and also critical process of moving in a new way. Hay spends much of her practice time exploring their implications and refining them for use in teaching. Each of her large group workshops has revolved around one of these directives, using it to provide the focus for daily movement investigations and for the final performance. For example:

> 1987: *I invite being seen drawing wisdom from everything while remaining positionless about what wisdom is or looks like.*
> 1988: *I imagine every cell in my body has the potential to perceive action, resourcefulness, and cultivation at once.*
> 1989: *I invite being seen not being fixed in my fabulously unique three-dimensional body.*
> (For comprehensive documentation of the workshops, see the list of performance practices included in this volume.)

Koan-like in their spare summoning of full attentiveness, these statements acknowledge the constant changing of body in consciousness.

Students in Hay's classes spend anywhere from forty minutes to three hours experimenting individually and collectively with one such directive as the generative principle and conscious focus for dancing. Throughout their exploration, Hay speaks very little. Rather than stipulate or enforce a specific way of doing things, Hay encourages students to investigate on their own, and interactively with others, the myriad movements the directive inspires. As the convener of this group exploration, Hay offers occasional new perspectives from which to continue exploration. If, for example, they are investigating "Alignment is everywhere," Hay might suggest the following ways of "playing" such a postulation:

> There is no one way alignment is everywhere looks or feels.
> The whole body at once is the teacher.
> Thank heaventz for the choice to play what if alignment is everywhere.
> Your teacher inspires mine.
> It doesn't matter if it is true or not. Just notice the feedback when you play it.
> Your practice informs my practice.*

Hay reminds students that they are teaching themselves by attending rigorously to the body's impulses. No body's responses will look the same. Each body can inspire others. All bodies can and should delight in the marvelousness of practicing dancing.

Compare this approach to dance training with a generic college-level dance class in either ballet or modern dance. Such a class stresses the body's ability (and inability) to conform to specified shapes at a given time. The technically proficient body is one that accurately and efficiently responds to the specifications. Embedded in each shape and limited to each temporal phrasing is a hierarchization of body parts, a valuing of parts in relation to a whole, through which the aesthetic ideal is conveyed. The dancer works to master these shapings and timings and, through the process, learns what the body can and cannot do. The body succeeds or fails, becomes recalcitrant or insufficient. It functions in reactive response to the will being exerted over it.

Hay's approach, in contrast, constructs body as a site of exploration to which the dancer must remain vigilantly attentive. Body does not succumb to the dancer's agency—striving, failing, mustering its resources to try again. Instead it playfully engages, willing to undertake new projects and reveal new configurations of itself with unlimited resourcefulness. Students receive no approval or criticism for engaging

*Hay explains that "These coaching directives formed during my experiences dancing with large groups of untrained dancers dancing." Personal communication.

in these explorations, nor do they learn to hate the body for its inade-
quacies. Rather, they orient toward body as a generative source of
ideas. Their reward comes less from mastering specific skills and more
from the sense of the body unfolding as a site of infinite possibilities.

The choreographic form of Hay's dances coalesces out of the exploration of these same directives. (Her renowned trilogy *The Man
Who Grew Common in Wisdom* developed from the three images for
1987, 1988, and 1989 cited above.) Increasingly attentive to what the
directive suggests, Hay and her students refine movement into similar shapes, repeatable actions, and identifiable phrases. For her large
group dances, Hay coordinates the individual contributions of all
participants, tuning them to the emerging score for the evening-
length piece. For her solo pieces, Hay often extracts impulses from
these variegated responses, sequencing them to suit a single body's
ability to elucidate the directive's shaping of physicality. While developing one of her dances, Hay may enact distinct images that specify a
shaping or quality of motion. But in taking on a shape or phrase, she
is not evaluating body's conformance to an ideal aesthetic. Rather,
she works to open all parts of the body—all seventy-five trillion cells
to the image, and at the same time she tunes to the dialogue between
body and image, listening for what each might say to the other.

Hay distinguishes between the practice of exploring the directives
and choreography in this way:

> They are two different animals. The practice is like the conscious
> heartbeat of the dance. The choreography is simultaneously the
> conscious choices I am making within the form.*

While practicing the directive, Hay makes certain choices and decisions, some of which she retains in subsequent practices so as to
build an established sequence. She does not mold patterns of movement in order to express an image, but instead, selects from her dialogue between body and image impulses that most vividly reflect and
amplify her experience of working with the image.

Once the movement material has been choreographed so that it
congeals in a reliably repeatable sequence of actions, Hay re-infuses

*Personal communication.

the performance of the choreography with focus on the directive. Using the choreographic form as a kind of stable reference, she re-animates each action with consciousness of the practice that produced it. Earlier in her career, Hay worked with several such images in the making and performing of each piece, moving from one to the next as the choreography progressed. Over a ten-year period of conducting large group workshops, she reduced and distilled her practice of images to a single meditation directive that now presides over and and focuses each evening-length work. Throughout the creative process of practicing, training, making, and performing dances, Hay continues to listen to the dialogue between body and idea. It is this cyclical listening process that *My Body, The Buddhist* documents so effectively.

Over the years, Hay's investigation of bodiliness has resulted in remarkably distinctive dances. In *Voilà* (1995), for example, the dancer performs a twenty-five minute solo full of startling non sequiturs that nonetheless cohere around a dream she recounts several times during the dance. She then reiterates fragments from the dance as accompaniment to her recitation of a description of each movement's intended meaning. In this diagnosis of the dance as part of the dance, movement's meaning explodes into a marvelous profusion of semiotic possibilities. Hay's analysis of each move shows it to signify both more and less than its conventional usage. *Exit* (1995), in contrast, elaborates on the dancer's focus, on the ability of body and face to project a sense of moving into past or future over a seven-minute cross from one side of the stage to the other. The stunningly simple structure generates multiple resonances around the word *exit*.

Hay's script of *Voilà*, included in this volume, provides a wonderful documentation of the diverse images contained within the choreography, and the changes to their meanings that result from sequence and context. It also challenges as it expands our notions of how to notate dance by calling attention to many of the ways that movement can be described and characterized. Having witnessed the dance first in silence, viewers then re-view the dance accompanied by verbal description, all phrased in the past tense, even though the speaking dancer performs them at the same moment she describes them. Viewers see movements from the dance isolated and explained, as if the spoken text revealed what the choreographer was "really" thinking. Yet the descriptions emphasize very different aspects of the movement, and their sequence is preposterously nonlogical. Hay refers to some of her actions in terms of their kinesiological components: "An arm poised el-shaped in front of her face. The wrist hung loosely." Other times, she emphasizes the metaphors movement can evoke: "She was a cartoon, playing horse and rider, but serious about the rules." A glass of water she is drinking turns suddenly into a microphone and then into a horse's tail. The varieties of description, the non sequiturs, and the use of past tense all unsettle the relationship between speech and action, underscoring the absurdity of the attempt to label movements, and ironizing the role of the choreographer as originator of movement's meaning.

At the same time, the talking creates a space full of conjectures and conjurings. It supports the dancer's restless exploration, the trying out and on of images. Both the dancer and the description mean differently at different moments. The viewer soon realizes that there is no real or deepest interpretation of the action, no message to be consumed. Calling attention to the relationship between location of iteration, whether spoken or danced, and its meaning, Hay's full-blooded irony plunges viewers into the experiencing and enacting of events while retaining a reflexive distance from them. *Voilà* stages a series of "what ifs" that encourages viewers to savor the process of meaning-making. In so doing, they may just learn that where they are is what they need.

SACRED DANCING

With respect to her own performances and also to dancing in general, Hay comments that the label "sacred dancing" is redundant. Dancing is always and already sacred in the way that it conjoins body and consciousness. Issues concerning religion and spirituality have permeated Hay's work for many years. In her writing she makes references to an eclectic group of religions including Christian, Buddhist, Hindu, and Jewish traditions. In her dancing she elaborates strong connections to the spiritual practices of yoga and the martial arts. Yet Hay's gestures toward religious experience have little to do with institutionalized worship or with New Age spiritual quests. Instead, she finds the sacred in looking at the daily through the lens of a cultivated physicality that is not being used in the service of anything else.

How does she look at the daily? and how does she maintain focus on physicality? As part of her training, Hay projects the existence of an observer who is watching her exploration of bodily cellular consciousness. Hay further projects a second observer who watches the first. Hay's moving body is thus watching itself moving and watching itself watching itself. Many theories of consciousness do not permit body to be consciously aware of its own activities while in motion. Many forms of prayer and meditation, even Buddhist meditation, encourage practitioners to sit and be still. In defiance of this opposition between action and reflection, Hay asserts the possibility of a consciously aware and critically reflective corporeality.

The best way to understand Hay's "sacred" dancing is to watch her dance or to participate in one of her courses. For those who want to imagine or remember her performance, *My Body, The Buddhist* offers a reading of body equivalent to her dances. That is to say, Hay's writing, never sentimental or nostalgic for a body that words only diminish, compartmentalize, or capture, crafts words with the same playful investigativeness that she implements in her choreographic process. This staging of a meditation on bodiliness, in all its devotion and doubt, deepens our understanding of dance and dance-making. Like her workshops, however, *My Body, The Buddhist* also makes the experience of physicality available to readers from many different walks of life, inviting them to share the dance.

acknowledgments

They are loved, the many friends in Austin who have supported my work with small and large favors that over time have become priceless gifts. Constant, whether I am away from Austin for long periods or at home, drawn to the comforts of my low profile apartment, these friends are essential to the network of relationships I need to live as I do. They are Emily Little, Phyllis Liedeker, Johanna Smith, Margaret Keys, Beverly Bajema, Will Dibrell, Claudia Boles, Diana Prechter, Sherry Smith, Ellen Fullman, and Eric Gould and Janna Buckmaster of Monkey Media. Michael Glicker has donated space for my solo performance practice at his Park Place Studio, for five years!

Just as consistent are my friends and colleagues in the field who make it possible for me to live and work in other communities near and far. These friends are Jane Refshauge and Margaret Cameron in Melbourne, Australia; Kris Wheeler, who housed me at her Whidbey Island, Washington, home for two summers while I worked on this book; Emily Day, another Whidbey Islander; Jana Haimsohn, the late Cynthia Jean Cohen Bull and Richard Bull, co-directors of the Warren Street Performance Loft in New York City; Elyse and Stanley Grinstein in Los Angeles; and Susan Foster of Riverside, California. All have sheltered me or provided me with access to their respective communities again and again. Movement Research in New York City, DanceHouse in Melbourne, and the School for New Dance Development in Amsterdam are institutions that have similarly helped integrate my work into broader community.

My brother and sister-in-law, Barry and Lorrie Goldensohn, included me in their winter and summer households for inordinately long stretches of time while I worked on *My Body, The Buddhist*. They were mercilessly astute with their feedback and editing. I thank them for standing beside me as an artist and sitting beside me at the dinner table as a family member, enriching me nightly. I am appreciative of Grace Mi-He Lee, who traveled as my master assistant during a west coast summer tour in 1998. Her presence in this role was stellar, and her editing tips were no less so. Rino Pizzi, a prince of a friend, also supplied invaluable last-minute editing advice. Scott Heron will always milk my soul.

Suzanna Tamminen, my editor at Wesleyan University Press, asked horrific questions of this manuscript. Her faith and belief helped me find the answers that she wanted and I needed to address.

I am grateful to Phyllis Liedeker, Todd V. Wolfson, Anja Hitzenberger, and Emma Hanson for permission to use their excellent photographs.

The individual artists who contributed a response to one of the eighteen chapter headings added immensely to the intention of this manuscript. I thank them, too, for bringing their fine art to life.

My daughter, Savannah Bradshaw, remains unparalleled in her effect on my living, breathing, and writing. I honor her here.

The inspiration for so much of the book's material was located in the dancing bodies of the following workshop participants:

⊘ for seven performers April 1993
    Beverly Bajema, Michael Arnold, Jewell Handy, Meg McHutchison, Grace Mi-He Lee, Jason Phelps, Ginger Rhodes Cain

Playing Awake 1995
    Polly Gates, Nicole Bell, Sarah Farwell, Charly Raines, Liza Belli, Elizabeth Kubala, Lisa Gonzales, Dorothy Saxe, Sylvie Senecal, Liz Gans, Angeles Romero, Genie Barringer, Harry George, Beverly Bajema, Colene Lee, Charissa Goodrich

Wesleyan 1995 Choreography Workshop
    Nicole Zell, Pedro Alejandro, Ara Fitzgerald, Sue McCarthy, Sara Kiesel, Christine O'Neal, Carla Mann, Joan Alix, Betty Poulsen, Hooshang Bagheri, Claudia Forest, Teri Roze

Playing Awake 1996
    Ellen Fullman, Adrienne Truscott, Rebecca Morgan, Kathleen Baginski, Mary Beth Gradziel, Edith Andermatt

Wednesday Nite Class 1996

Ellen Fullman, Adrienne Truscott, Rebecca Morgan, Cara Biasucci

Minnesota Dance Alliance Project 1996

Alexa M. Bradley, Thérèse Cadieux, Joan Calof, Janet Deming,
Mary Disch, Tara Arlene Inman, Susan McKenna, Sherry
Saterstrom, Susan Spencer, Karen Spitzer, Anthony Stanton,
Elena White, Laurie Young

1–2–1, Melbourne, Australia 1996

Anna Szorenyi, Bronwyn Ritchie, David Hookham. Hellen Sky,
Jacob Lehrer, Jane Refshauge, Karen Ermacora, Mandy Browne,
Margaret Cameron, Martine Murray, Megan Don, Pauline Webb,
Peter Fraser, Phil Mitchell, Anna Turner, Ranjit Bhagwandas,
Renata Bieske, Ros Warby, Shona Innes, Sylvia Staehli, Valley
Lipcer, Natasha Mullings, Adam Forbes

School for New Dance Development, Amsterdam, 1996 Workshop

Ivana Muller, Marianne Langenegger, Lianne Ernsting, Ellen
Kilsgaard Andersen, Katalin Balla, Katharina Pohlmann, Antje
Reinhold, Friederike Koch

Skidmore Workshop 1997

Judy Margo, Danielle Seymour, Kara Martinez, Jenny Thomson,
Megan Moodie, Abigail Sammon, Tracey Fischette, Nikki Verhoff

I am grateful to the National Endowment for the Arts Dance Program for its financial support of my work through its grants to individual choreographers. Since 1980 the development of my performance and dance practices would have been unimaginable without space and time secured with Dance Program Fellowship funds. Along with the generosity of friends and family, a 1997 NEA Choreography Fellowship allowed me to complete this manuscript.

I also wish to acknowledge support from the Rockefeller Foundation, the Kittredge Foundation, the City of Yarra, Arts Victoria, Australia Council for the Arts, the Minnesota Dance Alliance, and the McKnight Foundation in Minneapolis, Minnesota.

introduction

Alone in candlelight one evening several years ago I made a list of the most valued teachings learned from my teacher, my body. I wanted to itemize, to see a written account of the practical wisdom I have discovered while experimenting with my teacher as guide. Each of the eighteen lessons is a chapter title in *My Body, The Buddhist*.

When the inventory was complete, it spanned twenty-six years. I also noticed a parallel with Buddhist thought, although I am not a practicing Buddhist. For as long as I can remember I have intuitively preferred the politics of nonviolence. Nonresistance, seen in the bodies of many Buddhists, has always drawn my attention. And action through nonaction, at least as I perceived it on the surface, secretly appealed to my middle-class upbringing.

In the early 1970s, when I was living at Mad Brook Farm in Vermont, the books I was reading—in particular, *Be Here Now* by Baba Ram Dass and *Cutting Through Spiritual Materialism* by Chogyam Trungpa Rinpoche—advocated a spiritual path that was analogous to my experiences dancing. I was inspired to construct a verbal dance vocabulary that merged personal and universal images. I wanted it to include the sensual experiences of perception. With the help of language, I wanted to simplify access to dancing while expanding the territory from which a dancer could draw immediate kinesthetic experience.

Books and articles concerning Buddhist philosophy have proliferated in comparable measure to those written about the body. Yet I am certain that no two people living in a western culture would define in the same way either body or Buddhism. How we describe the body even changes several times a day for some of us. I have come to understand that the body's form and content are not what they appear to be; likewise, my dances do not coalesce around specific subject matter.

. . . once you have that experience of the presence of life, don't
hang onto it. Just touch and go. Touch that presence of life being
lived, then go. You do not have to ignore it. "Go" does not mean
that we have to turn our back on the experience and shut ourselves
off from it; it means just being in it without further analysis and
without further reinforcement. Holding onto life, or trying to
reassure oneself that it is so, has the sense of death rather than
life. (Chogyam Trungpa Rinpoche, *The Heart of the Buddha*)

My Body in the title of this book refers to a prescribed set of *what ifs*
organized around my work as a practicing performer, choreographer, and teacher: What if alignment is everywhere? What if your
teacher (your 53 trillion cells) inspires mine? Such imagined conditions, changed periodically, are necessary for me even to begin
dancing.

There has to be a certain discipline so that we are neither lost in
daydream nor missing the freshness and openness that come
from not holding our attention too tightly. This balance is a state
of wakefulness, mindfulness. (Chogyam Trungpa Rinpoche, *The
Heart of the Buddha*)

My Body, dancing, is formed and sustained imaginatively. I reconfig-
ure the three-dimensional body into an immeasurable fifty-three trillion cells perceived perceiving, all of them, at once. Impossibly whole
and ridiculous to presume, I remain, in attendance to the feedback.
At such times Deborah Hay assumes the devotion of a dog to its
master; reading the simplest signs of life, lapping up whatever nuance
my teacher produces. When the greater part of the Buddhist world
finds its strength, solace, and wisdom through a practiced devotion to
a guru, or Rinpoche, please imagine my hesitancy in admitting to
twenty-eight years of devotion to an imagined 53-trillion-celled
teacher.

The book grew from the list of eighteen statements that form its
chapter headings. But I did not write the material to fit the headings.
Several pieces had already been written when I began. Others I
wrote to help me understand and gain a wider perspective on how

dancing impacts my life and how life impacts my dance. With each story, or score, I would scan the table of contents until an unusually obvious or uncanny link to a chapter heading was made. The parallels were more experiential than didactic.

My Body, The Buddhist is the work of a dancer/choreographer not schooled in theory, analysis, poetry, or criticism. I study riddles, some of which are *what ifs* that arise when I am dancing. For example, what if where I am is what I need? As a dancer, I will notice what occurs when I *imagine* every cell in my body at once is getting what it needs moment by moment. The manner in which these *what ifs* can thrill and annihilate the body's reasoning process, overwhelming it with self-reflection, is similar to the experience of beginner's mind in Zen Buddhism. Dance is the field trip I conduct in order to interface with this experience.

It would have been antithetical to my process of inquiry to research Buddhist theory in order to substantiate my thesis. Long ago I stopped sitting at a desk surrounded by books, gathering information. My research happens in the experiential realm: dancing, standing on two feet, moving, listening, and seeing. I do not think people are going to read this text in order to learn about Buddhism.

I am not a practicing Buddhist. Nor am I a practiced poet, librettist, or archivist. The literary forms used in this book are liberties I have taken to help me unravel a piece of the plot between movement and perception. The libretto, poem, score, short story, were co-opted by a flag-bearer in pursuit of the study of intelligence born in the dancing body. I will try anything to help bring some attention to the truth born here.

My Body, The Buddhist describes innate skills and basic wisdom that bodies possess but that remain untranslated because as a culture we tend to hide in our clothes. Unrecognized is the altar that rises with us in the morning and leads us to rest at night. The book's intent is to open some trapped doors that prevent awareness of the body's daringly ordinary perspicacity.

Sixteen artists, of varied disciplines, were invited to illustrate a chapter heading with a drawing, a photo, or up to a paragraph of text. None of them knew the chapter content beforehand. It was positively uncanny to observe how the submissions received corresponded to the content of the chapter whose heading they chose. The result of their collective participation led me to believe that *My Body, The Buddhist* could as well have been titled *My Body, The Artist*. I find this parallel very intriguing.

my body, the buddhist

1 my body benefits in solitude

> I went to sit in a cabin on an ocean. There was a small boy
> there who was without a father. And we became friends. My
> desire to be without caved into his cunning child earth. My
> isolation forfeited, I meditated on his knowledge of knots and
> tides.
> — *Ralph Lemon*, choreographer

We are dying. We think we are not. This is a good argument for giving
up thinking. *Spend one night a week in candlelight.*

I lie on the floor in the corpse pose, called Shavasana in yoga.
*Wherever I am the dance is. Instead of dancing wherever I am, I choose the time
and space to play dance. This is equilibrium, and motion.* Several minutes
pass before I remember even to notice that my thoughts are going
yacketta, yacketta, yack—even after three thousand corpse poses.
*How many dance students dance alone uninterruptedly for at least forty minutes
daily, outside of rehearsing, choreographing, or physically stretching? Why is this
not a four-year requirement for every college dance student? How else can a person
develop an intimate dialogue with the body?*

Finally, I purposefully inhale and quiet my thoughts. *I hear a sprinkler
outside the window. Its pressure is low. Drops of water can be differentiated as
they contact the garden's surface plant life, its pillowy mounds and gravel paths. I
can almost feel the sprinkling of drops falling on me.* Thoughts begin to re-
duce in volume and appear at wider intervals. I make believe I am
dead because I am practicing the corpse pose. *There are three "what if"
components to the "I" who dances. What if*

- *"I" is the reconfiguration of my body into fifty-three trillion cells at once?*
- *"I" practice non-attachment to each moment?*
- *"I" know nothing?*

The weight of my bones, organs, muscles, and joints endlessly spreads out into the floor. *There are 206 bones in the human body, 26 in each foot.* Joints break open. Tongue dissolves. Throat disappears. I abandon holding onto the shape of me. *I am movement without looking for it.* Only a sketch remains on the floor.

I let go of the way my vision configures objects and perspective, trying to make things what I want or need them to be. *I see through a filter of what I know, instead of what I do not know, and so the awe is gone.*

I accept the fact that I cannot attain a perfect practice and instead use my energy to remember to engage the practice. In this way, I create futures I cannot achieve and then practice being here as the means for completing a day's work. At this moment there is always a forgetting of breathing, as if it were no longer necessary. The next inhalation is taken consciously. *Today while I was walking, the joint at the base of my big toe began to hurt. I did not walk last week and was trying to make up for lost time. I slowed down and steered my attention to the joint itself. It was tight and held. I spread my focus to include the bones, tendons, and other toes on the same foot, balancing the parts so the whole foot received the same awareness as the sore joint. I could feel the placement of my foot on the path relax and open. The joint was in pain as long as it was separate from the rest of my foot and the rest of my body. The pain lessened if I presumed I was in active rapport with an imagined cosmos.*

The more I unhinge the breadth of physical continuity, the clearer the sense of parallel lives, one of them just a silhouette lying on the floor. *What if there is no space between where I am and what I need? "Where I am is where I am" is reasonable, but less enjoyable than "where I am is what I need."*

Lying on my back, arms and legs slightly spread, in the corpse pose, I disengage all pretense, as much as possible. My synapses are no longer attracted, gone fishing, inactive, freed from bonding. A tinge of nausea compels me to persist. *Dancing is like going on a field trip. My body is the guide and tools, including the tape recorder. Last night dancing in my apartment I hardly moved and hardly needed to. I am not home unless I am in my art. I remember sitting on the side of my father's bed as he was dying. His hands were pressed together and tucked under his cheek, forming a small pillow for his head. There was a moment when I thought I saw him choose not to hold up the flesh of his face anymore.*

I am most of the time wanting to get something. That is why meditation is good, because I cannot meditate and get something at the same time. Meditation, as I use it to describe my practice, is not the correct word. You can't meditate and do anything else. I am not practiced at not wanting to get something. Now comes the thrill that awaits me in the corpse pose. It happens suddenly and, although I anticipate it, it requires full relaxation. It is very close to the ocean roar that occurs in the inner ear when a yawn is stifled. That roar feels like thousands of fluttering wings radiating from the center of my body. The sensation is brief but I am slowly learning to stretch it.

In a dream I tell composer Ellen Fullman that I just heard a concert of works composed by her good friend. She spins around and says "I missed it? It was tonight? How was it?" She responds with excitement, disbelief, and pleasure at hearing about it first hand. With equal enthusiasm, including tears that spread from me to her, I tell her the concert was great and that the crowds of people attending were so beautiful and they included all ages and races; that it was life and not racial diversity I was seeing. She knows and nods and together we appreciate what we do not have. When I am in the corpse pose I realize how much I hold onto life.

my body finds energy in surrender

Carolee Schneemann and Cluny, detail from Infinity Kisses, *1981–88. Photos by Carolee Schneemann, artist.*

I need a minimum of six months to choreograph a solo, and I have absolutely no interest in choreographing to music.

Playing Awake 1995 was a four-month movement/performance workshop for sixteen untrained and trained dancers, held in Austin, Texas.

It concluded with the premiere of *my heart* in April 1995. In May I began the most integrative phase of the choreography—extracting a solo from the group dance material. Seven months later, *Voilà*, born from *my heart*, premiered at the Public Domain, a theater in Austin.

Three weeks into the development of *Voilà* I knew it was a thirty-five minute dance—not long enough for a solo program. I decided to choreograph another dance, a short one, in order to have an evening's presentation, although the idea did not sit well with me. My group dances provided the foundation for all of my solo work. I was to be on tour with no time to make another group piece before the November performance dates. I'm attached to a self-imposed six-month minimum requirement for creating a new work. I am comforted by the multiplicity of assumptions held within any one of my beliefs.

Sur/Render was gathering force outside my walls. I can't quite believe its lordly presence in my creative process—thirty-odd years of bounty I could not have foreseen. Sur/Render, a warrior prince who, when summoned, rides a white horse into a mythic kingdom of possibilities. Sur/Render does not have to do anything. Its very presence attracts certain discrete elements that, when they arrive, gather substance as I explore and probe them. The new material integrates with previous elements in my dance-making process. Conjunctions are made. The body of experience deepens. After many years, my trust in Sur/Render has become viable and strong.

My decision to choreograph a new dance was coupled with a promise to myself not to think about the dance until it was absolutely clear what it would be, not to interfere with the compelling signals from the big void. For this reason I made no compromise in directing all my energy through that summer and fall to the choreography and practice of *Voilà*.

Voilà was demanding to perform because of an unusual combination of activity that included Italian speech, religious incantation, brazenly dramatic and contradictory behavior, and a lot of comic posturing. I knew it would, in turn, challenge the attention of its audiences. So, beginning the program with a simple, perhaps even an elegant, dance seemed smart. And getting smart was finally beginning to make sense. Give the audience time to arrive psychically. Do not destabilize them right off the bat. Surrender, please, some of the stubborn need not to entertain. Create a linear dance that might be attended to without effort. A beautiful woman in a beautiful dress. A flow of line and movement. A dance that does not threaten the ground that audience and performer have cultivated together for hundreds of years. Then, voilà, upset the apple cart after the fruit is served. The art of programming was dawning.

It was now late June. I packed my car with dance and outdoor gear and headed to the northeast to perform, teach, and visit my family and friends. The first stop was a choreography workshop in the Graduate Liberal Studies Program at Wesleyan University. My class met two and a half hours daily for three weeks.

Upon entering the studio, we placed our names beside a number that determined the order in which we would perform that day. For the first half hour, we collectively practiced the performance meditation *where I am is what I need, cellularly,* each student interpreting this phrase as it made sense to him or her. Then, following the list, each person had a maximum of five minutes to perform all or a selection of the particular work he/she was choreographing in the workshop. A bell signaled the end of five minutes. There was no pressure to complete the dance. The emphasis for the choreographer/dancer was to gain more insight into the material by performing it each day.

I proposed that, as audience for each other's work, we see each dance through the filter *where we are is what we need.*

At the sound of the next bell we had two minutes to write feedback. Two minutes later the bell rang again and the next person on the list performed.

After everyone's work was presented, the written feedback was distributed. The final bell signaled the last half hour, reserved for writing a personal account of one's own performance, including, or not, the feedback received. I was using the Wesleyan workshop to further unsettle the movement and my performance of *Voilà.* Any time more than one person described seeing the same image danced, I changed that movement or altered how it was performed until there was no trace of identical images left in the feedback I received.

The key to the success of the workshop was the bell. It kept us moving along with very little time to talk, forcing us to collaborate on meeting our own and each other's needs within the framework of class time.

During the same workshop, Christine O'Neal was choreographing a dance to the Molto Adagio from Samuel Barber's *String Quartet op. 11.* The music so moved me that each time she performed I became more convinced that my greatest challenge as a choreographer would be to use the seven-minute adagio for my new dance. I was about to surrender my second sacred belief, and the thought was so horrendous it made me sick. I knew I was on to something.

I had not choreographed a dance to music since Bob Dunn gave his 1962 composition class the assignment to choreograph a dance to Erik Satie's *Three Gymnopedies*. In my mind, the idea of choreographing to music bordered on coercion. I don't like being controlled by rhythm. I don't want any *one* outside influence to determine the course of the development or performance of my dances.

Toward the conclusion of the Wesleyan workshop another student danced one five-minute-long exit. That was how I saw it, and it briefly crossed my mind that it was a brilliant idea.

For the remainder of the summer I listened to Barber's Adagio on cassette, especially when I was driving. It evoked copious tears and loud cries. I called to my dead mother and father. I wanted to purge myself of my tremendous emotional response to the music so I could hear it better. What I could not abandon, and what undoubtedly contributed to the tears, was the terror of my commitment to this project.

On an early afternoon at the height of summer, I was running an errand and listening to the Adagio. I was driving, more like maneuvering, a narrow, winding dirt road in Cabot, Vermont. This two-mile stretch, through heavily wooded forest occupied by room-sized boulders takes anywhere from seven to ten minutes to drive, depending

Scott Heron performing in Exit, *January 31, 2000, Judson Memorial Church, New York City. Photo © 2000 by Anja Hitzenberger.*

on the weather. Just before the dirt road meets the gravel, the forest yields to serene rolling pastures, like a dress sliding from a woman's shoulders. At that moment, on that day, Barber's Molto Adagio came to its attenuated end and a new solo, *Exit*, was born.

3 my body enjoys jokes, riddles, and games

Standing at the precipice, I jump.
— *Ellen Fullman*, composer

SETTING: *The reader performs.**
Both hands are used to signal whether a joke, a riddle, or a game is being described. The reader will find this information in the margins.

A joke is represented by a raised right fist, thumb outstretched and bent at the knuckle. *A joke is something said or done to provoke laughter or amusement, as a witticism, a prankish act; an object of jesting: a thing or situation, or a person laughed at rather than taken seriously. Something that is amusing or ridiculous.*

A riddle is indicated when the tip of the index finger and thumb of the right hand form a circle. *A riddle is a question or statement so framed as to exercise one's ingenuity in answering it or discovering its meaning; a puzzling question, problem, or matter. A puzzling thing or person.*

When a game is described the left fist makes a quick knocking motion at an invisible door in space. *A game is an amusement or pastime: the material or equipment used in playing certain games.*

*Note: To prepare an audience for the reading, suggest that, while they notice the gestures and their application to the text, they also try to maintain the visual continuity of the two dances being described.

The group dance *1–2–1*, performed at DanceHouse, in Melbourne, Australia, in September 1996, contained a ten-minute sequence that strongly appealed to me right from the beginning. It was characterized by a tight, unpredictable musicality, suggesting acolytes in ludicrously formal worship.

I imagine every cell in my body has the potential to perceive Now Is Here—*a 1990s response to the 1960s cult adage* Be Here Now. *Now is the past, present, and future acknowledged as it unfolds each moment through each performer. Here is the awareness of that performer as he/she changes in relationship to the physical space, the other performers, and the audience.* The practice of this meditation was the primary focus of a three-week workshop leading to four public performances. The dancers applied the meditation to the performance of the choreography. The presence of a choreographed consciousness helped create an unseen landscape of relatedness among the all-Australian cast.

Twenty minutes into *1–2–1*, a short blackout concluded sequences of solo, small, and full group activity. Just enough light returned to the stage for the twenty-five performers to rise, walk to, and in the same moment complete, a square-shaped grid where each player faced at least one other player. The square was divided into two invisible triangles, Group A and Group B, with a common diagonal line from one corner upstage to its opposite corner downstage. Every dancer held two small rattles, one in each hand. The rattles were made from plastic vitamin, water, or similar capped containers with rice, salt, pebbles, or other small objects.

Stillness was broken by a short sound, neither loud nor soft, a single syllable that combined one consonant and one vowel voiced collectively by Group A. The sound initiated two events. Neither slowly nor quickly, Group A's arms rose overhead, holding the rattles still. Everyone in

Group B turned 180 degrees, quickly placing their rattles on the floor. The economy of the action almost erased it. Next, patterns that typically connect body to movement and sound appeared to be inoperable as Group B ungenetically traveled backward in a tight half circle around the inert rattles. The absence of timing, the limited use of space, and an overall appearance of bodies without pulse, pattern, or flow, created a visible coherency. Each dancer also produced short, one-syllable sounds that inventively evaded correspondence to the steps. Collectively, they orchestrated a deliberate interplay of monosyllabic music.

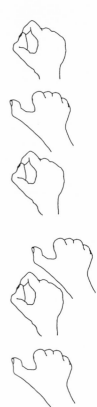

When Group A's arms arrived overhead, their rattles started to shake without fanfare. Quietly beating, the arms lowered. Halfway down, the rattling uniformly ceased, followed by a pause of indeterminate length.

A short, straightforwardly expressed, single syllable reinstated the descent of the rattles. The return of the light percussion cued Group B to abruptly halt its indecipherably deliberate anti-action. The dancers remained artificially rigid or bent in a position to reclaim the placed rattles from the floor. By the time Group A concluded its steady but not constant rattling, Group B had retrieved its rattles and everyone stood quietly.

An abrupt, unprojected monosyllabic sound, this time from Group B, started the sequence again in its entirety. Group A traveled backward around its inactive rattles; a tight, discontinuous dance with a lifetime determined by the coordinated rising of the arms of Group B.

When the sequence concluded, the entire group spontaneously re-divided into three parallel sections from up to downstage. The two outer sections performed the same material at the same time. The center column became Group A; Group B was identified as the bordering columns.

Group A began the same sequence as before, except that the space traversed by their ascending arms was now perceived astronomically, that is, it took a greater amount of time to cover the same amount of space without intentionally slowing the movement. Group B performed the single syllabic counterpoint to a backward, traveling, non-historical dance, but without placing the rattles on the floor, although a quick gesture, as if to leave them there, remained. Instead of dancing a limited path around rattles that were not there, they transited, performing the same movement, to the outer edge of the two columns, forming almost a line on opposite sides of the stage. When Group A began the imagined galactic descent of the arms, they were strongly featured stage center, beating their home-crafted rattles unobtrusively.

From its two semi-line borders, Group B simultaneously produced its one brief, unimposing call and then, without a tap from a rattle, the astronomically inspired ascent of the arms began. Group A, within their central columnar space, slowly congregated upstage applying a loosely disciplined counterpoint to their movement and single-syllable sounds. Group B, without aplomb, began beating their rattles, keeping them in the air above their heads while hastily converging on Group A, obscuring them from view like a door closing.

The audience was unaware of a conductor who, separated from and facing the group, directed all activity to instantly end. A fake falsetto liturgy began without any transition.

One month later in Amsterdam ...

With a small rattle in each hand, I move statically from pose to pose, speaking in languages of instantaneous origin, at times directed to or beyond the rattles. My body sometimes reflects the sounds produced. Gesture, voice, and movement, as they are applied within these parameters, are never fully realized by the performer. The challenge is

to maintain my alignment to the practice while juggling the choreographic limitations. *Every cell in my body has the potential to perceive* Now Is Here. *Now is personal. Now is past, present, and future acknowledged together as it unfolds each moment. Here is locating my changing presence in the physical space where I am dancing, including my relationship to audience.*

> What [Luce Irigaray] is claiming, by contrast, is that identity as understood in the history of western philosophy since Plato has been constructed on a model that privileges optics, straight lines, self-contained unity and solids. According to Irigaray, the western tradition has left unsymbolized a self that exists as self not by repulsion/exclusion of the not-self, but via interpenetration of self with otherness. . . . Forms are not fixed things, but temporary arrestations in continuous metastable flows, potentialities or evolutionary events. . . . The boundary of my body should rather be thought of as an event-horizon, in which one form (myself) meets its potentiality for transforming itself into another form or forms (the not-self). Such a body-boundary neither entails containment of internal forces nor repulsion of/protection against external forces. Those who are aware of themselves as centered "inside" an insulated container . . . are captured by an illusion generated by the mechanisms of ego-protection, as well as by spatial models inherited from a classical science which is now outmoded.*

Out of nowhere my palm collides with my chest, "BOOM," and reality shifts. Like a dart shooting from my body, my other arm strikes out in a straight line across my chest and into space. "TAAA," full of breath, escorts the

*Christine Battersby, "Her Body/Her boundaries: Gender and the Metaphysics of Containment," *Journal of Philosophy and the Visual Arts.* (The Body Academy Editions, Ernst & John, 1993).

arm. My mouth remains open as the force of the two acts continues in spirit.

Just before my enthusiasm is strained, the hand flips up at the wrist and the arm retracts at the elbow in a series of short jerks. An ordinary "ah," is spoken with each retractable jerk. The mouth closes between each "ah." In the middle of the last "ah" my arm rises like smoke from a cigarette on the lip of an ashtray. Before reaching its full height, the arm returns like smoke to the cigarette and I begin walking in a stylishly careful, easy, pretty manner. Partly because the rattle is not visible in my hand, the audience is unaware that I have invested the rattle with determining my path. I go where the rattle leads.

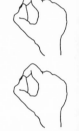

I step into place, a matter-of-fact "o" comes forth from my chest, and my arms rise out to the side and overhead. I imagine the audience has forgotten the rattles by now. The moment my hands are overhead the rattles reappear—not as rattles, but as two separate sounds produced from my hand or arm movement. Silence, the third sound component, separates and defines the two sounds. My arms descend, though they are not the focus of the action. The action is the sound and silence produced by movement and stillness.

Halfway through the descent, all overt action ceases. When I resume the descent, it is with the blessing of a very brief and ordinary "o." The descent complete, I quickly turn halfway and place the rattles on the ground. Following a tight half circle beside the two small objects, I attempt to undo coordination. Then I retrace the half circle, literally flowing. Bending to grasp my instruments from the floor, I hesitate anywhere and often before standing still in place.

In one hand I beat the rattle four times rhythmically. I repeat with the other rattle. I shake the first rattle continuously for the same duration as the four beats and repeat the shaking with the other hand. This rhythmic order is repeated until pattern is established. One rattle is then matter-of-factly stuffed into my shirt or pocket, and for a brief period I act as if it is still in my hand. The other rattle continues as if covering for its counterpart. Soon, the other rattle gets stuffed, and dancing has nothing to do with rhythm, and rhythm persists even after being removed.

4 my body engages in work

> When my body engages in work, it services the task at hand. It
> wants to be told what to do. My brain can't sweep the floor.
> Doing work creates the domain I want to live in.
> —*Susan Rothenberg,* artist

On February 15, 1996, I brought twenty-four tall, glass-encased candles, purchased at a Latino grocery store in Park Slope in Brooklyn,
into the dance studio at Skidmore College. I wanted to create a sooth-
ing atmosphere for the first evening seminar.* At the height of winter, the cool, blue glare from overhead incandescent lamps did not
add warmth to the innately bland space. In a storage closet I found
fifteen blankets, which I arranged in a circle in the middle of the
room. Circling them, I placed the candles. I knew that lighting candles on school grounds was not permitted, but I think everyone in
this country has reserved the right to ignore certain rules. I lit incense
and set up an altar, too.

The students, who were seated on the floor outside the studio when I
opened its doors to invite them in, were giddy with anticipation. It
was quite dark in the room. They oood and ahhhd. We were all ex-
cited. We performed solos in the candlelight. I cautioned everyone
about the candles because of the liquid wax forming at the top of
each glass. Two minutes into my own solo, I kicked over a candle,
which spread like a red sea on the gray-white marley floor. I felt

---

*Dance Chairperson Mary DiSanto-Rose and dance faculty member Toni Smith re-
sponded to a proposal that I return to Skidmore College to teach two seminars a week
for four weeks, each one based on a different chapter in *My Body, The Buddhist.* Since my
brother and sister-in-law, who are also my editors, lived in Saratoga Springs, where Skidmore is located, I could explore material with the students and get immediate literary
support from my family. Toward the end of negotiations, the dance department offered
to produce two evenings of my solo work at the Skidmore Dance Theatre.

ashamed, and hid my reaction with a decision to address the problem alone after the workshop. Some of the group noticed and stayed afterward to help. The numerous stains were obvious, as was the oily shine left after scraping off the surface wax. I would come in early the next morning and do everything possible to mend the calamity.

The next morning, in a mild panic, under the kitchen sink at my brother's house I found a plastic bucket and filled it with sponge, scraper, spatula, scouring powder, ammonia, a liquid abrasive, wire brush, and rags. Back at school, nothing worked. The woman who cleans the studio offered help, to no avail. I turned myself in to the lighting and technical director of the Skidmore Dance Theatre. We re-examined the damage, got an iron and placed it over moist towels, which absorbed the remaining wax stains, but we also managed to toast some surface areas. A custodian brought in an electric buffer and, whoosh, the floor was restored. For the following seminars I placed the candles out of dance range, trying still to offset the offputting cool blue glare.

In the fifth seminar, we explored *my body engages in work*. When the students arrived they found the twenty-four candles lit and grouped together next to a pile of blankets. The following directions were given:

> It takes forty minutes, traveling in increments, to form a triangle by following the length of one wall, the wall adjacent to it, and finally returning to your starting point through the middle of the studio. The traveling occurs individually within the group. It is possible, at times, to move significantly ahead of the others but a return is necessary. Your attention and command is helped by remembering, "What if every cell in my body engages in work?" You have forty minutes to examine this query. This is the dance, performed collectively—a hive in action and focus. There is no one way the work looks.

> The practice, *my body engages in work*, is offset by a secondary practice of nonattachment to any one way you are working. Thus you are not required to be logical or continuous in one kind of activity; nor are you compromised by the time, space, or work of others. In this regard it is useful to read each other as cellular

entities engaging in work, rather than, "I wish I was home," or, "What is she doing?"

Every performer is responsible for moving her two articles: the blanket and the candle. You move each article forward, in increments of space and time, in any combination, order, frequency, duration. You choose when, how, and where to move, while staying within the parameters of the group and the overall spatial pattern, more or less.

Work-related activity with the blanket can be opening it, folding it, spreading it out, holding it up, wrapping it around, carrying it forward, or piling it up.

Work-related activity with the candle can be carrying it forward, lifting it, lowering it, or moving it along the floor.

I chose composer David Dunn's *Angels and Insects* (Nonsequitur Recordings) to accompany the dance project.

After the group received its instructions, I reminded them to be aware of the candles. It was the first time they were reintroduced into the dancers' immediate vicinity. Five minutes into the dance the first candle was capsized, by Abigail, whose face lifted in a red panic. I quietly alerted everyone to gather where Abigail was sitting. Like bees, we worked the wax up from the floor, scraping it under our fingernails—which was possible because the wax was still mushy and warm. We pushed the wax off our fingernails, back into the glass candle or into our other palm. Our hands moved quickly, adeptly, and in silence we worked until all the wax was gone. The green dye did not have time to bleed into the dance floor. Time did not rule. No thoughts distracted us. Five minutes later a second candle spilled, and without saying a word, the work we had done earlier began again.

The students' feedback, immediately after the dance, follows:

My touch completed what was already in motion.
Multiple experiences are possible with permission.
Nothing was left out of my experience.
Gravity is a wonder.

Darkness makes friends with the light.
My cells quest for activity.
I felt spontaneous without trying.
I am not as limited as I feel.
Separate parts come together.
No one stopped until it was completed.
So many hands in one area.
No one in the way of others.
Looking down at the hands was like seeing slow motion.
A satisfied deliberate quest to make a difference.
It was focused, centered, determined motion.
Seeing something and finding myself doing it before it becomes a
plan. Including others made it easier.
It amazes me how much interest and intensity I felt.
When I knocked over the candle I thought "O my god," but then
I thought, "Oh good. We all get to come together again."

5 my body commits to practice

> My body commits to practice Robert Wilson.
> —*Robert Wilson,* artist

Each new performance practice signifies a conscious re-invention of my mind. Beginning with a puzzlingly simple feeling of integration experienced while I am dancing, I attempt to articulate and then devote myself to exploring and measuring the consequences of this fleeting logic. When I have discovered all I can from one approach, I move to another.

I feel like a tower of babble. Millions of voices speak from my body at once—no one voice more dominant—a deliberate exercise to outwit the need to encapsulate. Tower is the continuity of my performance. Babble is the energy. Why Tower of Babel? What was it I learned in Sunday school forty-five years ago?

> Now the whole earth had one language and one speech. (Gen. 11:1)

> Come, let us build ourselves a city, and a tower whose top is in the heavens; let us make a name for ourselves, lest we be scattered abroad over the face of the whole earth. (Gen. 11:4)

Late one morning I was walking with my daughter around Town Lake in downtown Austin. We noticed people standing looking up at the sky so we stopped to see what they saw. The sun was a pale white disk behind a much larger circle of gray matter that resembled oatmeal, or brains. A ring of bright sunlight radiated around the edge of the circular gray matter. The sight was ominous to me, because until that moment I could more or less account for what occurred in the skies. We stayed and watched as an airplane flew past, leaving a jet stream that bisected the celestial event.

The local public radio station was jammed with callers wanting more information about the morning's solar event. Within minutes I learned that we had been looking

at a meteorological halo. I sat down to draw it, realizing it was the symbol I needed
to publicly identify my current dance play with seven characters.

Indeed the people are one and they all have one language, and this
is what they begin to do; now nothing that they propose to do will
be withheld from them.

Come let us go down and then confuse their language, that
they may not understand one another's speech. (Gen. 11:6–7)

Draw a circle with a fine pen or sharpened pencil on an empty sheet of paper. In
the process, remain relaxed and notice how the circle is forming on the page. Before
completing the circle, without lifting your pen from the paper, draw a second circle
just inside the first one, as if you are giving the inside of the first circle a shave.
Maintain a noticeably restful mind. To finish, join the end of the second circle with
the beginning of the first one.

Lift the pen from the paper and look at the circles. Choose a place inside, other
than the center, to draw a smaller disc. Without breaking the motion of the pen,
darken the area of the smaller circle until it is completely opaque.

Hold the pen like a slicing blade. Draw a straight line traversing the double circle
at any plane on the opposite half of the circle from the dot. Begin and end the same
distance from the edge of the circle from points outside its circumference.

The symbol you have drawn identifies a dance play I choreographed in 1993. By
substituting a symbol for a title I was asking the audience to enter a movement-
based world without clutching the few words that usually help mediate ap-
proaches to art. Even the title, untitled, implies something about a work and its
author.

So the Lord scattered them abroad from there over the face of all
the earth and they ceased building the city. (Gen. 11:8)

The traditional interpretation of the Tower of Babel episode is that it
is about judgment and punishment. For trying to reach God through
material means? Because what holds us together must be beyond language or place?

The *tower of babble* became the first of my performance practices to
incorporate the past and future in the present. The traditional interpretation of the Tower of Babel was not the one I danced. It wasn't

to punish mankind that the tower was destroyed. I propose that it was destroyed as a challenge to humans to independently locate god consciousness within. As such, it activates the radical in me. Affirm the revolution within the individual, celebrate the community of differences. Art effectively replaces historical shortsightedness by creating a different future in the present.

First I remove physical height from my perception of tower. Tower is where I am in all of my pretense, belief, control, and absence of control. The Tower in The Tarot of Paul Foster Case is "the mouth as the organ of speech. It breaks down existing forms in order to make room for new ones."

The dance was identified by an index finger circling two times, then all the fingertips of the same hand clustering together and vibrating in a single location inside the invisible circle, followed by the fingers releasing and the index finger bisecting the imagined circle and stopping. This was going on all over town, wherever members of the cast or friends of the dance company spoke about the new piece.

I practice remembering my toweringly singular dance: the rightness of nothing much, including absurdity and the choice to surrender anything that wants definition. On the other hand are the rigor, exactitude, and the thrillingly subtle music of the moving body.

Babble is the sound of a single voice. Babies babble. Tower is babble. Babble, tower. I talk nonsensically. I sound like a schmuck. I change accents, scream like a maniac and hear the toweringness of my babble leave my mouth and travel out in space. Everything I hear is complete, whole unto itself. Language and voice lose meaning. There is only music.

Babble has no identity beyond itself. *Tower of babble* is the perfection of chaos.

"Pnkk."

At these times my body chooses not to wander. Imagining every cell perceiving the toweringness of every discontinuous moment, unique, and whole, is more varied, revelatory, and concise than endlessly flitting thoughts.

In the Playing Awake 1993 workshop we exercised the choice to perceive each other's dance as towers of babble. Our thread was not a tenuous one. We were reinventing tradition in a prescient context that was binding. Our imaginative bodies seemed inexhaustible.

Their personal intent is visibly cohesive and pure. Four sets of barefoot toes ultimately appear under each woman's hips.

Tower is a metaphor for consciousness. Babble is the reality check. The Tower of Babel is a metaphor for performance. Tower is the attention. Babble is each moment of movement.

This Tower of Babel is a constantly shattering, nondiminishing tower. Perceived as inseparable, tower/babble creates a self-induced continuum of attention.

Imagining fifty-three trillion cells at once, with the potential to recognize their toweringly fleeting lifetime, is the practice exercised by the seven dancers in ⌀

It is difficult to describe her actions. It doesn't seem to be necessary.

6 my body seeks comfort but not for long

> The past is irretrievable and the future doesn't exist. Why don't
> I remember this more often?
> —*Michael Ventura*, writer

In February 1995, Linda Montano asked seven Austin dancers to participate with her and Ellen Fullman in a seven-hour memorial for her guru who had recently died. Linda used her voice in memory or celebration of each of the seven chakras. Ellen Fullman played her long-stringed instrument, an installation consisting of 120 strings, each eighty-five feet long, suspended from wall to wall and played while walking and stroking lengthwise with rosin-covered fingers. Both women performed continuously for seven hours. The event was held at The Candy Factory, Ellen's studio, which housed the long-stringed instrument.

Linda invited each dancer to choose a chakra they wanted to explore. (As explained by Hindu and Buddhist texts, the chakras correspond to glands associated with human behavior.) Our choices were:

5–6 PM	*ovaries/testes—sex*
6–7 PM	*pancreas—security, money*
7–8 PM	*adrenals—courage*
8–9 PM	*thymus—compassion*
9–10 PM	*thyroid—communication*
10–11 PM	*parathyroid—intuition*
11–12 AM	*pituitary—joy, bliss*

I chose the thymus, the heart chakra, the experience of compassion. I had recently heard the Dalai Lama talk about the importance of compassion and it left me wondering what specifically was missing from my personal identification with it as an attribute. This was an opportunity possibly to find out.

From what I understood about human interaction, I felt the need to experience compassion for myself before I could extend it to others. Dancing alone the week prior to the memorial event, I became aware that I do not, as an experimental artist, bother to feel love and acceptance of the self who is dancing, or of the self who has danced for fifty years. It is not that respect, acceptance, and love are absent, but that these experiences have never been the subject or object of my dance inquiry.

Except for a slight distinction, love and compassion are the same. Love involves the wish that beings be happy and affirmed in their lives. Compassion is the wish that all beings be free from suffering and/or its causes. The wish to be free from suffering is practically the antithesis of being an artist. In a letter to Agnes DeMille, Martha Graham said, "No artist is pleased. There is no satisfaction, whatever, at anytime. There is only a queer, divine dissatisfaction: a blessed unrest. . . ." Could I turn this around, if only to see what it would feel like, for the sake of the memorial for Linda Montano's guru?

The evening of The Candy Factory Memorial Celebration was cold and rainy, the studio uninsulated and damp. The room was long, narrow, and painted black to highlight the long-stringed instrument's copper-colored harpsichord strings, which took up three-quarters of the space. The audience capacity was thirty, and that night we were twenty at most and not for long. People came and went over the seven-hour period. Those who stayed were wrapped in blankets or bundled in their coats. I was to perform from 8:00 to 9:00 P.M., following the ovaries, pancreas, and adrenals. I watched Beverly Bajema perform the sex chakra. She wore lipstick-red clothing and sat on the floor with her back to the audience, curled forward, moving very little. We were left to imagine the range of her evident and complete attention, maintained for an hour. From a distance, deliberately letting the bodies of audience members come between myself and Beverly's performance, I was seeing and not seeing the event before me, like drinking soup from a bowl, feeling its effect without looking directly at it.

At 7:45 P.M. I stepped into a cold, dark bathroom along one of the long walls of the studio. I could not turn on the light because it would disturb the performing area. I stripped off my warm clothes to put on a green silk blouse and shiny green culottes. My nipples were raisins, my feet cold as ice, and my skin unresponsive. Shivering and cranky, cursing the day I accepted the invitation from Linda, I wondered what in hell I was doing in the middle of Texas on this wet, frigid night with twenty people sitting on the other side of a black door. Just before eight, I stepped out of the bathroom and saw Linda sitting cross-legged on a dais at one end of the room with a cloth over her head, wearing sunglasses, and wailing into a hand-held microphone. Ellen, in a dark suit, was patiently traversing the length of her strings, holding them between her thumb and index finger, creating tones I never hear otherwise. Suddenly everything was clear. These dingy, hard-to-find, derelict locations in every major city on earth are sites for the brewing of an art chemistry that cannot be produced any other way. I need that alchemy and the twenty or so people who also need and support these exotic laboratories of experience.

Before them, I invited being seen free of all suffering and its causes, including my garish green costume, the site of the ceremony, the constancy of my collaborators in the seven hours of ritual, the karma of those gathered that night in The Candy Factory. Teetering on the brink of idiocy, still I did not abandon the practice. If this was compassion, then I had to laugh at the distance I keep from the love that issues from this kind of inclusiveness.

Why, since that night at The Candy Factory, do I not return to that dance?

At the end of Woody Allen's film *Bullets over Broadway*, the once aspiring playwright, exhausted and elated, returns to his wife and says, "There are two things of which I am certain. One is that I love you and two is that I'm not an artist." "I am not an artist. I am not an artist." I don't know what possessed me to replay those words again and again, as I sat in the theater. It felt as if I was part of a fake cleansing ritual. Purity herself went running through my veins. My teeth would have walked away from my gums, from the freedom this thought implied. "I am not an artist." I wished I meant it, but knew I didn't.

7 my body is limited by physical presence

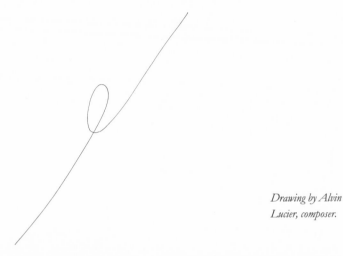

*Drawing by Alvin
Lucier, composer.*

A dance is choreographed. It is performed. If a dancer or choreographer is lucky, there will be several public performances. Most dances have a weirdly limited lifetime. The hours I have spent on stage performing dance add up to less than a single year. My body is limited by physical presence. I need more from dance than what I can get dancing. In 1988, a Laban Institute graduate offered to translate *The Gardener* into Laban's system of dance notation and analysis. *The Gardener* is the second in my dance trilogy *The Man Who Grew Common in Wisdom*. A month later, she handed me the notated dance, admitting to critical choreographic omissions because of elements in the choreography that did not have a counterpart in the notation system. At that moment dance documentation began to interest me. Video and film, done in a way that could approach the mystery of live performance, was out of my price range. Writing dances began to open the boundaries of my personal experience of dancing. I discovered that prose would help determine how my dances were transmitted.

When I write about the physical act of dancing, unique assemblies of thought often occur. These thoughts often reinform my choreography and performance. My body as performer is more inclusive in the aftermath of writing a dance.

For example, the concluding movement in the dance *Voilà* follows the recitation of a story told twice at different intervals by the solo dancer.

> A man dressed in medieval hunting clothes grabs a small bird by its tail feathers. He presses the tip of its tail firmly onto a table. As the bird frees itself, some of the feathers remain on the table and scatter. The man turns to me and says, "This means looting."

The soloist circles the stage, galloping, and exits through the theater rather than into the wings. By the first public performance, *Voilà's* man/bird story had become a parable concerning all art as looting. The transformation of a bird into feathers symbolized the artist/alchemist turning one element into other. Feeling a bit smart, definitely poetic, and not at all limited by my physical presence, I circled the stage and exited, the final image of the artist-as-looter.

A few weeks after the premiere of *Voilà*, while creating a dance libretto, I described the end of the solo this way:

> She began galloping in circles [following the story-telling]. A horse, rider, woman, playing, dancing. A human being galloping off. [This is how I leave stage.]

Reading the first line evoked memories of charging horses. I was trapped by two wild mustangs who had broken through their fence and at top speed began circling the house where I had been working on *Lamb at the Altar: The Story of a Dance* (Duke University Press, 1994). They would break stride and prance right up to the front door, nervously pressing their bold heads against the screen before jerking back to their hostage-taking antics. The panic they aroused in me, by their physical presence, annihilated mine.

In the second sentence, I realized that horse, rider, woman, playing, dancing, human, being, and galloping, could all happen at once. I was no longer limited to the body of the artist. My theatrical persona could expand to include this cross-pollination of the collective unconscious. My galloping became less serious. I found greater distance from the actual shape of the dance being performed, yet I felt more substantial. I realized that in those first performances, my body *was* limited by its physical presence.

I decided to memorize the fifteen-page dance libretto and perform it as text—a performance piece of a performance. I had no trouble learning the lines and this was satisfaction enough for entering into this development of the dance material. I began to practice the text in a choreography workshop that I was conducting as well as participating in. For fourteen weeks, each of us presented solo material from an individually developing work-in-progress. During these sessions I learned from the group that the performance of my writing continually held their attention as audience. I also noticed a wide range of interpretations of that performative writing.

Most startling was hearing my own voice intoning a powerfully archetypal command of *Voilà*. The dancer, galloping in circles and exiting, had become almost inconsequential.

She Began
Galloping in Circles
Horse
Rider
Woman
Playing
Dancing
A Human
Being
Galloping Off

8 my body knowingly participates in its appearances

It is beyond dispute that no character in fiction, even if conceived as an ape, a beetle, a fantasm, is without connection with real persons experienced by the writer within contact of sight, sound, and touch, or second-hand through experience recorded by others in one medium or another, and whether or not the writer is always aware of this. . . . For this creature, formed from the material and immaterial—what has breathed upon the writer intimately, brushed by him in the street, and the ideas that shape behavior in his personal consciousness of this time and place, directing the flesh in action—this fictional creature is brought into synthesis of being by the writer's imagination alone, is not cloned from some nameable Adam's rib or Eve's womb. Imagined: yes. Taken from life: yes. What do we writers have to work on as looters in that fragmentation of the possibilities of observation, of interaction, of grasp, in the seen and unseen, constant flux and reflux, the conscious and unconscious defined as "life"?

—*Nadine Gordimer,* writer

VOILÀ, A DANCE LIBRETTO

SETTING:

The prologue is read aloud by the choreographer, who is sitting at a table with a quart-size jar of water. While reading, she intermittently stops to drink.

PROLOGUE

Eight performances of *Voilà* ran for two consecutive weekends in November 1995 at the Public Domain, a performance venue on Congress

Avenue, three blocks from the state capitol in Austin, Texas. The theater was on the second floor of a two-story building. Its aesthetic similarities to performance lofts in New York City were a comfort to the choreographer. Three days after the performances ended, the choreographer packed her bags and flew to Acapulco to visit a friend.

Four days into her Mexican holiday, she began writing a dance libretto for *Voilà*, but before she started, the dancer felt compelled to document three Acapulco street scenes witnessed the day following her arrival.

Scene One: At a crowded market, on one of the narrow, crumbling sidewalks busy with the very poor, an old man stood holding himself upright with one hand pressed into the doorway of a women's clothing shop. He seemed dazed, although it appeared he wanted to get inside. Black cotton pants circled his ankles. No other clothing covered his body. His slightly yellowed skin was sprinkled with brown spots and scabs. The area around his coccyx was hollowed out. Aside from a few schoolchildren who stood off giggling, no one stopped marketing. The American choreographer thought that maybe the old man's daughter owned the dress shop.

Scene Two: On the return to her hotel, from the window of a taxi at a busy crossroads at the edge of the market, she spied a barber shaving an old man angled backward in the barber's chair. His bony head, at the end of a skinny neck, lay turned toward the street. The rest of his body lay hidden by a white sheet. Pleasure radiated from his closed eyes. He stayed that way.

Scene Three: From the balcony of her eleventh-story hotel room, she was transfixed by tourists who departed the sandy beach via a parachute pulled by a speeding motor boat. For ten minutes, a flyer would drift above the bay and shoreline, secure in a harness fitted to the flyer's chest. She could feel her own body lifted, legs dangling, heart trembling, pulled through space. Her fascination included the memory of a photograph of her daughter, who made the same leap years earlier. That photograph, turned upside down, had become the title page for the choreographer's dance score, *The Aviator*.

THE MAN WHO GREW COMMON IN WISDOM

part III THE AVIATOR

choreographed and performed by Deborah Hay
original sound score by Ellen Fullman

PREMIERE SEPTEMBER 8 & 9, 1989   AUSTIN, TEXAS

dedicated to my daughter Savannah Bradshaw

Title page from The Aviator.

The original draft of the libretto was written under a glass-domed ca-
bana on the roof of an historic building overlooking Parque Mexico
in Mexico City. She wrote at a small table beside an unused swimming
pool on which specks of plant life alone floated. The house was
rented by the Australian Embassy for one of its government employ-
ees. Rebecca, a young, vivacious correspondent for the embassy, lived
in luxury on the first floor. The choreographer's friend lived in a small
room on the ground floor. He was a permanent guest in Rebecca's
house because his conviviality and warmth made it a more welcom-
ing place for everyone who visited there.

The libretto was further developed at the Hyatt Regency Hotel over-looking the Bay of Acapulco. Televisa owned the hotel and employed her companion as a main character in *Acapulco Bay*, a soap opera that was being filmed in both Acapulco and Mexico City. She followed her friend back and forth between the two cities over a twelve-day period.

At this point the choreographer removes her reading glasses, rises from her chair at the table, and moves around the stage using her body as a reference for the spoken text.

I.

She remembered prancing forward.

Across dance floors, from one corner to its opposite, her pointed feet barefooted.

Voilà, she entered prancing sideways, clipped and poised.

From darkness into light she side-stepped urban memories of horses.

The back of her body pressed close to us, suspending perspective.

Horse-inspired movement ceased mid-crossing, replaced by her clucking mouth.

She clacked, and clicked horse walk, trot, canter, gallop, and prance.

The sounds swept her into horsey locomotion and dance.

But she was stopped by a wall.

Caught with her pants down.

Fini.

Done.

Why end what had just begun?

What would she do while the audience watched her back?

How long would she stand here?

When the questions ceased she began again.

"Uno," danced. ("Uno" because she loved Italian and would soon be visiting Italy.)

Combining movement, gesture, mime, and a little more Italian, she philosophized on oneness.

She cried "Bravo."

Then she threw in "Brava."

To subdue her enthusiasm for Italian she whispered "Madonna."

"'Madonna.' She tried it in three different virgin poses." Voilà. *Photo © 1997 by Emma Hanson.*

Madonna had nothing to do with her liberal Jewish past.

"Madonna." She tried it in three different virgin poses.

"Basta."

Enough!

Italian?

"Basta."

Nothing . . .

"Basta."

Nothing stretched between three to four bastas.

"Abbastanza . . . . . . ," the last of the bastas was dead serious.

She spun once, tight and fast, 360 degrees, gathered upright.

She traveled evenly from side to side in various five-step combinations.

Step-together-step-turn-step (to the right).

Step-turn-step-together-step (to the left).

Each step and turn was accompanied by a short sound, almost a syllable.

She fixed on one that drew her to a specific invisible something somewhere.

She found a semi-apparent glass of liquid.

Bending to grasp it with the right hand, she lifted it from the floor.

The glass, above her head, was tipped toward her lips, which did not open.

Her body drank enormous quantities.

The glass became a microphone.

She, a reporter, related the following story as if it were incontrovertible truth:

"She found a semi-apparent glass of liquid. Bending to grasp it with the right hand, she lifted it from the floor." Grace Mi-He Lee in Voilà. *Photo © 1997 by Tom Brazil.*

"She found a semi-apparent glass of liquid. Bending to grasp it with the right hand, she lifted it from the floor." Voilà. *Photo © 1997 by Tom Brazil.*

"She found a semi-apparent glass of liquid. Bending to grasp it with the right hand, she lifted it from the floor." Scott Heron in Voilà. *Photo © 1997 by Tom Brazil.*

A man dressed in medieval hunting clothes grabs a small bird by its tail feathers. He presses the tip of its tail firmly onto a table. As the bird frees itself some of its feathers remain on the table and scatter. The man turns to me and says, "This means looting."

II.

The hand-held microphone became a horse's tail.

She galloped in circles, changing styles while retaining a sense of ritual.

From the circles came angular, heraldic, mighty, big steps.

Arms crossed the body in sweeping motions.

Fingers were spread. Elbows erect. Her torso arched upward.

The dance went strongly forward.

Then she retraced and widened the path just made.

Brief flashes of movement sprang and were retracted so quickly she appeared surprised and wondered in their aftermath.

A foreshortening of the body galloping ensued; a comically pretentious rhythmic gallop.

"The dance went strongly forward." Voilà. *Photo* © *1996 by Todd V. Wolfson.*

An arm poised el-shaped in front of her face.

The wrist hung loosely.

The other arm was a limp tail wagging.

There were brief pauses to change arms, look around, rock back and forth.

This made everyone including herself half believe that what she was doing was really something.

She was a cartoon, playing horse and rider, but serious about the rules.

She rode three sides of the periphery.

The metered journey ended beside a four-foot-high, black cylindrical stand.

Its diameter was wide enough to hold a small bronze bell.

Her back to us, she took the bell with her left hand and drew it to her chest.

The theater was still.

Farts were blown from her loosely secured tongue-parted-lips.

Saliva spread in the theater light.

Faint body movements reflected the fart noise.

The effect of the farts on the audience eventually subsided into silence.

One chime from the bell broke the spell.

The ringing was heard disappearing.

She licked the back of her right hand between thumb and forefinger.

Pressed to her mouth, blown upon, she produced a new series of more contrived fart sounds.

Saliva sprayed.

Silence reigned.

For the second time a single chime interrupted and faded to stillness.

The bell dropped and she dropped to a squat during the third variation on the fart.

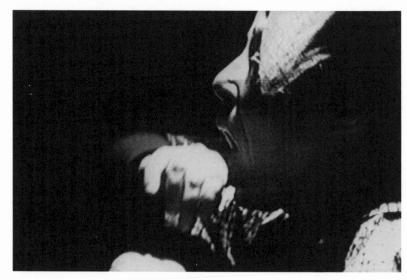

"She licked the back of her right hand between thumb and forefinger." Voilà. *Photo © 1996 by Todd V. Wolfson.*

A wordless song, a vein from ancient Judaic culture rose to fill the theater.

Her torso, head, and arms gesticulated upward.

She teetered exaggeratedly.

Wildly jittery crooked fingers poked upward at the air.

Slowly turning to us was a dwarf-like burning songstress.

The song quit mid-note as abruptly as she had dropped twenty seconds earlier.

The primitive jarring dwarf dance continued swiftly and in silence.

Without a beat lost she rose on tiptoe.

Her fingertips met and formed a circle above her head.

Her feet returned to the floor. Looking at her body as if for the first time she repeated the story told by the reporter, only she spoke as if she were seeing a dream:

"... she spoke as if she were seeing a dream." Voilà. *Photo* © *1996 by Todd V. Wolfson.*

A man dressed in medieval hunting clothes grabs a small bird by its tail feathers. He presses the tip of its tail firmly onto a table. As the bird frees itself some of its feathers remain on the table and scatter. The man turns to me and says, "This means looting."

III.

She recalled one of her robot movement memories.

Left arm/right foot, right arm/left foot forward she marched.

Each step matched a reconfiguration of her pursed lips through which she sent air spurting.

She stopped before us and placed a forefinger handgun into each hip holster, the two gestures highlighted by brief lip blasts.

Two guns whipped back out, forefingers aimed, thumbs erect, fusillade sprayed.

Few survived this oral exercise.

Returning each forefinger to hip with a short blast from her lips, the frozen march resumed.

Halting, she swerved back blanketing us with machine gun fire.

The robot strode away.

Pivoting around, she lunged forward keeping her back leg strongly grounded.

Her right arm, bent at the elbow, rose heroically. Its position brief but established.

We were given several views of the right arm crooked and aloft.

The movement repeated more or less on her left.

Torso and head curled forward as both legs came together.

With false effort she lifted something vague and nonimagined into the air. This took time.

Little catch steps carried her to a downstage site.

With arms crossing and uncrossing at her heart, she crafted the briefest of sighs while arching upward and bending forward.

Her right hand stopped at the pubis.

The fingertips moved up the front of the body in broken stretches of time.

She serenaded the passage with deliberately uninspired atonality.

At her hat's tip the hand and body made one quick tight turn in the air.

She was sent hopping backward on one foot and the other.

The free leg hung or dangled.

Forward stretching arms acted like rudders steering her backward and away.

Suddenly the full force of controlled passion came racing toward us.

A notable rhythm drove her.

Directly in front of us, possessed yet controlled, she rushed right to the edge.

Left, to her limits.

Right again.

Left again, maintaining the strict rhythm of the dance.

She turned, containing herself in a hideously ornate position.

A variety of rhythmic steps zigzagged from right to left, near to far.

Her second journey along the same path was less controlled.

Bleeps and shrieks flew from her mouth as efforts to contain herself were applied.

By the third trip she lost it.

Rhythmic constraint was shot.

Choreography disintegrated.

Guffawing and stomping, she spent the passion that remained.

We noticed her comfortably tucked into a distant corner.

Leaning unfamiliarly, she stood quietly facing us.

(A man in a barber's chair outside the Acapulco market.)

Carefully traveling, she lifted and lowered one or both straight arms and/or legs.

She switched, repeated, opened, closed, and crossed the same pairs of limbs.

She sank onto one knee, then the other, until the tip of her hat touched the floor.

She drew a line straight backward away from us.

There was time to appreciate the absence of strain or design.

Behind the hat's tip a body narrowed and lengthened facing the floor.

Behind the tip of a hat she turned over onto her back.

As her body energy released, both legs and arms shot upward.

Her lower legs dropped independently in increments.

In the air her knees changed direction and her legs spread partially.

Her torso rose from the floor as if it could stand itself up.

"Carefully traveling, she lifted and lowered one or both straight arms and/or legs." Voilà. *Photo © 1997 by Phyllis Liedeker.*

"Carefully traveling, she lifted and lowered one or both straight arms and/or legs." Voilà. *Photo © 1996 by Todd V. Wolfson.*

Short whines were produced.

Unaware of her intent, her costume and hat prominent, she got to her knees and turned to us.

When her face lifted, the brief whines ceased.

Her hands were spread fan-wise, one above the heart, the other above the belly.

Not fixed, they had a life of their own.

Three times the lower face dropped as the upper part lifted, dividing her face at the nose.

The return to normalcy was like going to the store.

Rising directly to her feet from the third facial distortion, her facial normalcy returned.

Clustered touching fingertips on each hand met the tall hat inches above her temples.

An angel approached.

"Three times the lower face dropped as the upper part lifted, dividing her face at the nose." Voilà. *Photo © 1997 by Emma Hanson.*

An angel turned, becoming an elder leaving.

Halfway gone she paused, turned back, and an angel returned.

A hand dropped from its place on the hat to grasp an invisible microphone.

The man/bird story was retold with a flamboyantly sorrowful French Canadian accent:

"Clustered touching fingertips on each hand met the tall hat inches above her temples." Voilà. *Photo* © *1997 by Emma Hanson.*

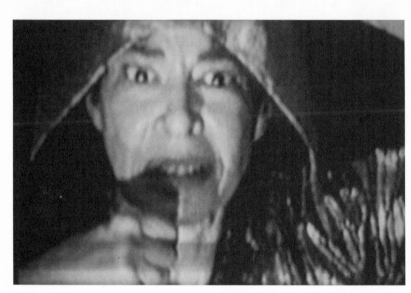

"The man/ bird story was retold with a flamboyantly sorrowful French Canadian accent." Voilà. *Photo* © *1996 by Todd V. Wolfson.*

A man dressed in medieval hunting clothes grabs a small bird by its tail feathers. He presses the tip of its tail firmly onto a table. As the bird frees itself some of its feathers remain on the table and scatter. The man turns to me and says, "This meeesurmpphh."

The last two words were swallowed by the artist's body.

IV.

She began galloping in circles.

Horse rider woman playing dancing.

A human being galloping off.

Backstage, her animal friction vanished with the choreographic form. Numb and tired, delicately tethered to her bones, an adrenaline-motored flight lifted the dancer for hours.

The Kitchen presents **The Voilà Project.**

Deborah Hay choreographed Voilà then wrote a dance libretto which she sent to **Scott Heron** and **Grace Mi-He Lee** who, over this past year learned Voilà exclusively through the prose score. Other than the libretto, the information shared is the length of the dance and the same performance meditation practice. All three artists will perform their own staging of Voilà each evening.
Sue Poulin, lighting designer, is the only collaborator who has knowledge of all three dances.

April 3-6 8pm $15
The Kitchen, 512 W 19th St.
Call 212-255-5793 to reserve.

Postcard design by Scott Heron.

"There are the movements, occurrences, tasks, tricks, and traps that constitute each dance. These actions take place in the experiential realm. Then there is a substructure, an exercise not unlike a meditation, that is applied uninterruptedly throughout a dance. The substructure is a set of conditions that exists in the imaginative realm. It unifies, through practice, the sequence and performance of the dance material. Without the substructure there is no dance."—Deborah Hay

9 my body likes rest

> I can be embraced by the very core of who I am, quite still.
> —*Eva Karczag*, dancer

I received help. October 1, 1996, a driver of a black sedan, courtesy of the Rockefeller Foundation, met me at Malpensa Airport. I had left Melbourne, Australia, twenty-four-and-a-half hours earlier. After fifteen months on the road, my luggage was too much to cart anymore. I was carrying performance and dance practice clothes, street and dress wear for all climates, my powerbook, printer, and needed business papers.

My arrival in Italy was preceded by six weeks of teaching and performances in New Zealand and Australia. In Melbourne, I had premiered *1–2–1*, a dance for twenty-four people. We worked from nine in the morning until six at night for ten days, and then gave three public performances. Every morning before nine, I was in the studio practicing my solo, *Voilà*, which followed *1–2–1* on the same program. Our last performance had been September 28. On October 3rd, I would start a month-long collaborative artists' residency with Austin artist Tré Arenz at the Rockefeller Foundation's Bellagio Study and Conference Center. I was tired. I had planned two days to wind down and empty out before starting this new project.

The driver suggested we take secondary roads instead of the highway. I thought I would see farmhouses and vineyards, villages and gardens; life among the real people. But business was booming in northern Italy. Young women prostitutes stood by the side of the two-lane thoroughfare, trucks and cars whizzing by, waiting for a chump. Roadside advertising blurred my vision. Lumber, wire, steel machinery, concrete blocks, and stones lay piled or stacked ready to be formed into industrial warehouses or showrooms. My breathing, in general, was slowed and disturbed by the foul air from car and truck exhaust and the degradation of the earth's surface in sight everywhere. The competition for space was unyielding. I gradually froze with fatigue.

Months earlier a reservation had been secured at Hotel Belvedere, a moderately priced accommodation in the town of Bellagio. Upon arrival, I learned that the man who occupied the room reserved for me had become sick the night before and I would have to stay in a flat a few doors down the street and a few flights above the local movie house. I could move back to the hotel after the man's son came to fetch him. I traipsed up three flights of stairs to check out the appropriated flat. It was light brown. The only light came from a small, inaccessibly situated skylight. The woman at the reception desk back at the hotel tried to pressure me into this disappointing alternative. She did not share my fantasy of the restorative right setting—one that would satisfy a single woman alone on the shores of Lake Como for the first time in her life. I had imagined a small sunlit room with a little balcony. Flowers. A lake. Cappuccino.

I left my bags and went into town to check the other hotels. All were booked, except for the five-star Grand Hotel Villa Serbelloni, situated at the tip of a peninsula on the Lago di Como. (The summer camp I went to for ten years was on Lake Como, in Pennsylvania.) They offered off-season rates. I was shown room number 265. Opposite the foot of the bed was a floor-to-ceiling window that faced north, away from town and onto the lake. Downstairs, the sitting rooms that divided the main floor were stupendously luxurious. The grounds were diverse and peaceful. The town lay at its doorstep. I stood at the desk for a half hour, one side of me pleading with the other to book the room. "You are out of your mind." "What do you mean?" "You cannot afford this hotel." "When will I have an opportunity like this again?" "Who do you think you are? You could live for almost a month on what you would pay for this room." Ad nauseum.

From my window, across the Lago di Como, the mountains, shrouded in fog, appeared and receded in a gray haze. On the bed was a white terrycloth bathrobe wrapped in clear plastic with the insignia of the Grand Hotel Serbelloni over a breast pocket. I took a short bath in a long enamel bathtub that narrowed at the bottom like the hull of a ship. Afterward, I lay on my back on top of the sheets, under a leg-long comforter, the bathrobe snug and secure around me. The window was open. Lago di Como lapped at its shores. It chomped when ferry traffic passed. It was a mesmerizing rest. I felt my body reconfiguring itself evenly, at an almost dizzying constancy. On one hand, I was perfectly still, and on the other, I was arriving, from Australia, flying into and catching up with my prone body.

A few hours later, I went for a walk in the garden and then returned to a drawing room with all varieties of antique chairs, couches, and tables arranged for tête-a-têtes and small groups. There were gold-leaf candelabras, marble pillars, parquet floors, oriental carpets, ornately framed paintings and mirrors, and floor-to-ceiling curtained windows that doubled as doors that could open onto a broad verandah. Potato chips were served with my tomato juice and, because the sitting room was empty, the sound of the chips breaking apart in my mouth seemed unbelievably noisy. A man seated in a far corner was served potato chips with his drink, too. As if they were trying not to be heard, three musicians in black suits played the piano, bass, and violin. When I went up to the room to change for dinner I lay down again and had that same sense of sliding into and away from dimension. A strong intent to arise was required in becoming vertical again. Dinner was at eight and I was very hungry. My last meal had been breakfast between Bangkok and Rome.

The tall ceiling and the antique white and gold decor of the dining room reminded me of a mirrored ballroom where I performed in 1981 in Antwerp, Belgium, the same year I danced at the Festival d'Automn in Paris with poet and percussionist Bill Jeffers. Replacing his voice and drum was the same violin, bass, and piano trio, now playing with more gusto. Instead of dancing I was now eating in a dining room with three long rows of round tables filled with couples. The waiters were fabulous to watch. Quick, curling wrists and decisive serving hands moved with finesse to and from the tables.

The sun set, leaving a clear gray-blue light. Palm fronds blew left outside the large glass-paned windows in the same drawing room where

I had eaten potato chips earlier. I was incredibly happy—the need to just be, and be grateful, to not speak, or think, was being resplendently sated.

A storm raged through the night but I was barely disturbed behind the thick shutters and windows of room 265. It was biologically consoling to feel so protected by the quality of this turn-of-the-century architecture.

The next day I took a long walk following narrow alleyways, many bordered by stone walls supporting the life of the most delicate white flowers. I wasn't making decisions. I returned to the hotel and with my Powerbook Duo 2300c found separate sites for writing; first the verandah, then a bench closer to the lake, and finally a sundeck chair looking out onto a view of the mountains that drew me away from writing—it wasn't hard—and into a multifaceted peacefulness. I was unaware of the depth to which the visual experience of harmony was being absorbed.

My two-day respite was hauntingly complete. (I can feel how that harmony has altered me.) Part of it was the majesty of the Grand Hotel itself, but a greater part were the mountains, the lake, the small towns crimped to the shores and spotting the mountainsides, the gentle winds that invisibly wove the cypress and olive trees together. The light etched the mountain tops and ferries slid across the water; moody church bells intermittently rang from undisclosed sources near and far. The same three musicians returned again and again to set up their instruments—piano, violin, and bass—to entertain the guests.

After dinner on the second evening a married couple were the only ones dancing in the drawing room. They danced to the music of the three-piece band. The man was a good deal taller than his blond wife. He held her close and I enjoyed watching how he exerted just enough pressure to her back so that her breasts familiarly met his chest. But it was the man's dancing feet that attracted me. Every so often, coming out of a slightly dashing turn, he would elongate the lower part of his leg clear to the shoe tip. In contrast, he emanated very little above. To notice this delicate maneuver, this elegant aftermath, this little accent at the tail end of his body, danced, was a sign to me that my rest was over.

10 my body is bored by answers

> my body likes the levitation in questions
> —*Robert Irwin,* artist

I was never drawn to participate in sacred dance classes. I feared my irreverence, cynicism, and snobbery. Little did I realize that my problem was linguistic. Sacred dancing is redundant.

11 my body seeks more than one view of itself

> Each morning I drink a most feared view. I let in EVERY VIEW.
> My body fills, absorbs, distills. Is Still. I'm going to be an
> uncontained container, a transparent vessel, an invisible mist.
> Everyman. I'm going to dance a new, fuller-bodied
> *Disappearances* [barely visible outdoor dancing for New York
> City, 1994].
> —*Douglas Dunn*, choreographer

Dying has become a vital component in my performance practice. Attracted to the ephemeral, I have explored dying for years.

So I wasn't surprised when praying surfaced. As far as I know, very few of my peers have been smitten with similar holy journeys within the context of experimental dance. It is generally understood that we veer away from this subject matter altogether. Finding myself with the task of exploring spiritual values in the avant-garde dance world has not made my teaching or performing profession easier.

Is praying, like dying, relevant to my human as well as dance vocabulary? How was I going to ask students to join me in this movement exploration? The thought made me shudder. Many students dropped my dance workshops when they heard the word prayer. I would have, too, in their shoes.

The practice of praying is difficult to approach directly. The word *prayer* seems to suck the energy right out of many people, including myself. I tried replacing it with some other term, to distance it from its historic, cultural, social, and personal associations. Freed from those encumbrances, my cellular body presented an alternative approach.

Praying became a dialogue with all there is.

Praying arose in the same manner as my other dance exercises. *I am alone dancing and for a few moments my body is caught in an aching sense of depth and connection. I want to know I can revisit here, and so the desire to articulate my experience momentarily replaces the dancing.*

With pen in hand, I sit and listen and record what I believe my body is recreating for my conscious mind. It is usually a single thought, in the form of a paradox, or a riddle. I then construct a network of conditions which guide my approach to examining the riddle or thought. Not in search of an answer, I kinesthetically gather evidence from the feedback. After several months to a year of practice, I can sensually embody the riddle or thought without having to deconstruct it first.

I pray—not to anyone, not about anything, and not for answers. Certain other conditions need to be in alignment;

- *creating time each day for uninterrupted attention to its practice,*
- *reconfiguring the self into fifty-three trillion cells in an active, nonlinear "dialogue with all there is." "Dialogue" requires my participation and it balances the lightness of "all there is." I believe my cellular body knows dialogue in a way that I rarely experience in ordinary life.*
- *I presume dialogue is present and I exercise the choice to notice it. I do not create, look for, or try to define it.*
- *I endow my cells with this ever-changing exchange with anything I can or cannot see.*
- *I do not burden myself with the veracity of the exercise.*
- *I imagine that what I see—the trees, sky, dogs, people, river running—is dialoguing with every cell in me. My noticing dialogue describes how I see rather than what I see. It attaches me to my universe.*

Praying is thus liberated from content and replaced by a peaceful alertness.

I am alone in a canoe under a blue sky in Vermont. For the first time I experience breathing as a *dialogue with all there is.* I think of my mother, who was chronically ill throughout most of her life, and the following poem arises:

From my heart. *Left to right: Charissa Goodrich, Beverly Bajema, Sylvia Senecal, Angeles Romero, Lisa Gonzales. Photo © 1995 by Phyllis Liedeker.*

"As I galloped, for instance, I could choose from a library of gallops I had witnessed for four months." Angeles Romero in my heart. *Photo © 1995 by Phyllis Liedeker.*

"As I galloped, for instance, I could choose from a library of gallops I had witnessed for four months." Voilà. *Photo © 1997 by Tom Brazil.*

I was afraid
if I breathed too loud
you would be disturbed or die.

My lungs are passive
in fear of losing you.
I breathe alone in my body.

Prayer is my window out of breathing alone in my body.

When I pray under these conditions my body's boundaries dissolve. I am replaced by my breathing. My lungs are paper lanterns. My bones feel alive and my mind porous. Peripheral and depth perception bristle with input. My body senses integration with its immediate vicinity. I experience generous and fundamental well-being. This is how I can participate, understand, benefit from, and value praying.

How can prayer be performed in western culture without its boring men, women, and children? That was the personal as well as collective challenge in the Playing Awake 1995 workshop in which *my heart* was choreographed and from which a solo dance, *Voilà*, was later distilled.

I watched the dancers in *my heart* perform for four months, imagining they were practicing prayer, without knowing that that was what I was seeing. After the public performances, from the first day alone in a studio deciphering what was to become my solo *Voilà*, I felt like living proof of the transmission of prayer. As I galloped, for instance, I could choose from a library of gallops I had witnessed for four months. It was more than the gallop; it was the spirit of the person dancing that gallop. It was as if I had been handed a fully formed experience, without the loss of any part, and I could move into it, play alongside it, and ultimately emerge finding my own way onward.

12 my body delights in resourcefulness

Her work brings to body a meeting of comedy and tragedy in
the absurd order of the unconscious mind where meaning is
courted, suggested, betrayed, denied. Its meaning exits and
enters in the same movement along the same road and asserts
its conclusions in an unknown language conveying a sense of
both clarity and arbitrary meaninglessness in the same gestures;
with a hysteria that proceeds from an inner calm that finds it
amusing; with an inner secrecy that finds it all-revealing; with a
sense of serene orderliness in which it does not seem to matter
which arm or leg will move in which direction or sequence, and
which conveys a sense of urgent flight as slowly as she can move.
— *Barry Goldensohn*, poet

FIRE, 1999

PART I

It is dark. A light pops on in the distance. A woman without a
stride walks into this light. She pauses, determining when to
enter the flow of the dance; to jump into the river.

She starts in the middle of the dance. Precision her passage;
a chisel the closer she gets to me. The timing is complex; an
overture of moments within the decline of lived time. We, the
audience, see a portion of her.

She turns (I don't see her turn) and asks, "Who are you?" My
worlds break.

"Where are you from?" she slapsticks boxes with physical
geometry. I swim to shore.

"What do you want?" is sincere. "Fire," she breathes. "What do you want?" again. "Higher!" A wasteland song is captured, tightly burning. A chaos chanting in her body fixed to a linear path.

There is a sudden unmarked shift in her trajectory; a woman walks toward me and then retraces her approach. The burning transit continues.

Her heart swells.

She decorously circles.

She makes a second circle (which is not a circle, although it is her intention that it be a circle) and performs adhering to some form of inner logic, like an acrobat on the high wire.

With passion and gusto the woman slips into a theme and variation on a dance triplet, extenuating the conclusion of Part 1.

PART II

The scale of the physical space is now opened to us through a bond between the woman's tense visceral dance and its passage along the outermost circular boundary of the stage.

She cries singing, coming toward me, turned away.

"Who are you?" she croaks with fear, having twisted around to look at me. Loud anxious breaths are beats that pound at my body.

"What do you want?" is rasped in alarm, and an uncommon aftermath of hollow pants parts the air.

Doors close crashing shut before her. This she gestures while pulling up from inside her the sound of these offenses that slam in her face.

A gurgling rises up and out through her throat and mouth. Water ruptures the frozen doors. Her arms, a barricade across her chest, gradually loosen.

Buoyed and floating out into a slow sprint she moves forward. Turning her head, now and again, we sense her being followed. What follows catches up with what is before her. She is squeezed into consummation in the moment.

She wakes and lightly steps forward as if crossing the street in a foreign city; looking at us but seeing stars in the sky.

She begins talking to an imagined lover sleeping a short distance away. Something like the following words are spoken: "Get up baby. I want you to see the stars. They are so beautiful tonight. Come on honey."

Her lover rises. He is represented by the palm of her left hand rising, facing her. Her right palm approaches her left. This is to be her. She says "Thanks baby. I am so glad you are up." The palm lovers glide to the front of her body and turn to face us. They sigh at the sight of the stars. They turn to each other, nod, and look back at the stars. They shift to her right side and become a telescope.

Holding the telescope in both hands she looks at the stars, slowly traversing space. She remains focused and concentrated while lowering the telescope. She looks up, but continues the movement of the telescope toward her navel. She speaks: *"She swims to shore. A chaos chanting a wasteland song. Before the master she lies face down, mouth open, fire. Like a baby in the presence of its mother, she burns."*

Although she no longer looks through its lens, the telescope is now pointing directly to her navel. Heat generates. She burns. We are struck by her response. In a single gesture, her hands separate—the telescope vanishes. She steps backward, away from us. We see fire as the lights go out.

She is looking for a job, her preference is to work on a one- to two-year performance project with an inspired, innovative theater director. A generous annual wage would compensate her commitment to explore the body as a window onto metaphysics, myth, pathos, humor, sound, history, horror, ordinariness, poetry, nature, and dance.

She is not a trained actress but a conspicuously alert performer. She invests her cellular body with unparalleled perspicacity, not to inflate her ego, but to explore the imaginative body. She shuns outside stimuli in favor of infiltrating trillions of cellular entities with perception.

She has experimented in this particle-sized dimension for more than twenty-five years, finding it to be an unlimited source for personal and artistic feedback.

She is unafraid of performance intimacy because she understands she is not the object of its allure. The momentary is her muscle.

To dislodge a performance pattern she devises movement instructions that are not attainable through logic. Relatively speaking, this causes a violent disruption of an habitual energy field—favoring the state of curiosity that arises from inquiry.

She likes to juggle. Instead of balls or batons, she practices with four or five perceptual experiences at once. She drops balls but it doesn't matter. She retrieves them when their absence is noticed. The director should know she prefers juggling to catching the ball. There is no time to capture or translate when someone is juggling. This freedom from knowing arouses the curiosity that precedes question-making. And this is where she feels performance lives.

The choice not to work with a mirror forced her to develop her own monitor of her presence. Several years ago, she was in residence at a college for the arts. She wanted a place to practice alone before teaching and was given access to a ballet studio. A shocking realization occurred as she stepped inside. Here was a room, representative of thousands like it around the world, where people of all types, but particularly the young and vulnerable, came to dance. Waist-high horizontal bars bisect these studios. When students first enter, they are already conditioned to grasp those bars for support. Self-identification and awareness are sought in wall-size mirrors. A sticky, powder-like substance called rosin is spread on these floors so the dancers' feet do not slide out from under them. What assumptions are implied about the people who come here to dance?

How did the absence of mirrors in the place where she danced strengthen her performance skills? She learned to project another self out from her body, but turned facing herself. Whole and changing, she invited being seen by the projected witness. After some years, she projected a second witness, even further out and looking from a different perspective, who could see her seeing herself being seen. With the help of these witnesses, not only did she become more alert and aware, she was able to make choices about how and where she was in space and how and when she appeared in time. An uncanny thing happened as a result of imagining these witnesses: it seemed that the more places she could project herself, the more intimate her dancing felt.

The inaudible voices of the moving body, surfaced through writing, have proven to be an asset to her career as a dance artist. The alliance with an inspired director will therefore include writing their collaboration. What is the context that brought them together? Where and when did the movement toward one another begin? What conditions were in place to make this happen? And then, what would be their chemistry together? Where would they start? How would their separateness merge? What would they come to understand about each other's work? And, how would they personally relate? How would their collaboration assemble itself? What would their collaboration create? What would become the essence of the collaboration? How would they impact each other's future?

Interested directors may contact the artist here.

13 my body trusts the unknown

> Because I have taken my body, by my will, to so many
> unknown, strange, demanding and frightening places, it is no
> longer afraid.
> —*Linda Montano*, artist

The I Ching, an ancient Chinese book consisting of sixty-four ora-
cles, was the single source of guidance to which I referred for choreographic direction before the start of my four-month workshop,
Playing Awake, 1995. To consult a hexagram, three coins are tossed in
the air six times. The combination of heads and tails determines
which of sixty-four oracular messages one consults. How I have
interpreted the hexagrams has profoundly changed the course of my
life. In this instance, the tossed coins fell to the hexagram *Following*,
changing to *Gathering Together*. *Following* contains these messages: "The
thought of obtaining a following through adaptation to the demands
of the time is a great and significant idea . . ." and "No situation can
become favorable until one is able to adapt to it and does not wear
himself out with mistaken resistance."

The word "adaptation" had never crossed the threshold of what I
believed was my vastly inclusive artist's consciousness. I could even
say that, until that moment, my dances had been choreographed and
staged according to stringent principles of nonadaptation.

The first day of Playing Awake 1995 I asked everyone to perform a
short solo with the following guidelines:

1. the dance could be performed anywhere in the studio,
2. no preparation was necessary,
3. there was no need to be creative.

I took notes. Each solo contained moments of eccentric and moving

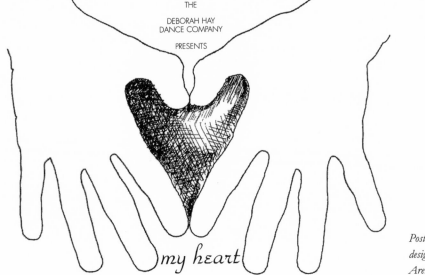

THE

DEBORAH HAY
DANCE COMPANY

PRESENTS

my heart

Postcard
design by Tré
Arenz.

material. A few days later, I asked everyone to prepare and perform a
monologue about something that aroused their passion. They had
three days to write and practice before presenting their monologues
in the workshop. My reasoning was that, given these two assignments
early on, everyone would confront their worst fears about performing right off the bat, and, hopefully, they would recognize the value
of the performance tools I would then be offering them in the course
of the workshop.

It was not my intention to manufacture the rich supply of resources
from the solos and monologues that inevitably became the structural
continuity of *my heart*. Nonetheless, I selected from and adapted the
material, which, in turn, sped up and eased the choreographic process. *my heart*, the name I gave the dance to help me remember mine,
was frightfully simple to paste and put together choreographically.

The implementation of "adaptation" was not without its cost. I knew
I was using the students' work for my own ends, and I suffered recurrent bouts of guilt.

Six weeks into the same workshop, I had the following dream: A
man dressed in medieval hunting clothes grabs a small bird by its tail

feathers. He presses the tip of its tail firmly onto a table. As the bird frees itself, some of its feathers remain on the table and scatter. The man turns to me and says, "This means looting." The message I interpreted from the dream was that holding onto anything, for example my students' creative bounty, was looting.

The structure, imagery, and clarity of the dream was so haunting that I included it, as text, in *my heart*. Two different performers told the story at different intervals. Not being skilled in dramatic arts, they found it difficult to pronounce "looting" without over-articulating it. It being the last word in the story further compounded its troubling pronunciation: "looting" became the focus of the story. I listened to my dream repeated twice a day for over three months. It wasn't exactly like being hit over the head.

In a letter to my brother, I described what was happening. He sent back a T. S. Eliot quote: "Immature poets imitate; mature poets steal . . . The good poet welds his theft into a whole feeling which is utterly different from that from which it was torn." Reading this, I felt much better, although the guilt did not disappear entirely.

Five months later, while choreographing *Voilà*, the solo form of *my heart*, I discussed the dream with my dream group, seven women and a Jungian-oriented psychotherapist. I read aloud from my dream journal and then described what was happening in my life at the time of the dream. I spoke about the hexagram *Following* and my struggle with the concept of adaptation as far it concerned my art. The group leaned inward. I was asked to describe the man in greater detail. I said he was large and gentle and wore heavy, richly textured clothes. His face was courteous beneath his pointed hat. He may have been an alchemist. When he said "This means looting," he lowered his voice and opened his arm toward the scattering feathers. As I made this motion with my arm, this, referring to the feathers, replaced looting as the subject of the story for the first time.

This is adaptation, transformation, integration, art, and life.

His lips flap, blowing air.
He turns red. Spit on his face.
He grovels, grunts, signs and moans,
bends his body to fart, shit, explode.
He disappears
in his juicy gases.

She is embarrassed, belittled,
caught in the middle of the wrong dance.

Lisa Gonzales, standing; Polly Gates, sitting; in my heart, *1995. Photo © 1995 by Phyllis Liedeker.*

A chorus line chants
and dances, undoing
their monosyllabic trance
one by one.

Left to right: Liza Belli, Sarah Farwell, Lisa Gonzales, in my heart, *1995.*
Photo © 1995 by Phyllis Liedeker.

A woman
approaching tentatively,
joins the man with a black hat, and fake beard.
Her hands saddle his shoulder.
She perches by his ear
and breathes song here.
This moves him.

Dorothy Saxe and Harry George in my heart, *1995. Photo © 1995 by Phyllis Liedeker.*

She wears a red and gold satin dress. She is a horse (from any angle). She is a woman who is a horse.

"It hits me. The smell. It's sweet, rank, pungent. It lingers in the hairs of my nose. I sniff and remember something from way back. I mean way back, from before I was separate. It's in my blood. It's an almost unbearable feeling of homesickness. My eyes drink everything in. I wait. The luster, the lights. The hush. The smell. The first clown enters and ring and I am gone."—Liz Gans

Liz Gans in my heart, *1995. Photo © 1995 by Phyllis Liedeker.*

A woman strides on stage. Black cape with fuchsia lining.

"Sorry to hold you up."
She removes an imaginary pair of socks.
An angel stands at the door of her house.

Dorothy Saxe and Sylvie Senecal in my heart, *1995. Photo © 1995 by Phyllis Liedeker.*

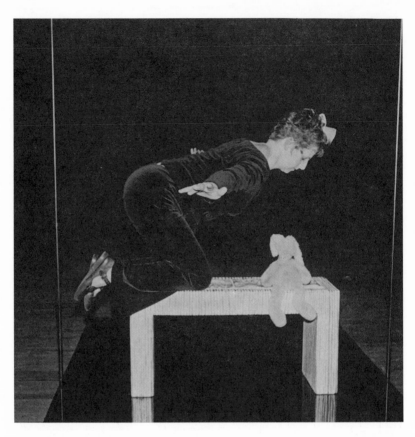

at home by a bench

a girl and a rabbit play
and wait
prayers escape

Charissa Goodrich with her toy rabbit in my heart, *1995. Photos © 1995 by Phyllis Liedeker.*

14 my body feels weightless in the presence of paradox

> My working method has more often than not involved the
> subtraction of weight . . . I have tried to remove weight from
> the structure of stories and from language. . . . Maybe I was
> only then becoming aware of the weight, the inertia, the
> opacity of the world—qualities that stick to writing from the
> start, unless one finds some way of evading them . . .
> Whenever humanity seems condemned to heaviness, . . . I have
> to change my approach, look at the world from a different
> perspective, with a different logic and with fresh methods of
> cognition and verification.
> —*Italo Calvino*, writer

Exit is seven minutes. Samuel Barber's Molto Adagio from the String Quartet, *Opus 11, played by the Emerson String Quartet, inspires the solo dance. As the lights come up, the performer is seen standing to one side of the stage. The impulse to begin moving comes after the music starts. An arm lifts in the direction the dance will travel. The dancer crosses from one side or corner of the stage to its opposite; the arm leads or follows the body. There are three or four opportunities for the performer to turn back and face in the direction where the dance began and herein acknowledge her past. The time it takes to cross the stage and exit corresponds to the length of the Adagio.*

When the music starts the dancer hears an appeal to exit. In so doing, she notices she is also entering. The two experiences are as inseparable in life as they are occurrences in her body. The weight of the past mingles with the weightlessness of becoming. The combined consciousness of these two equally moving events splits her into tremors of responsiveness, and she hasn't even taken her first step.

Her focus on a single destination is removed from every square inch of her journey. The historical role is to project one's vision into the wings, where a demi-god (the future) sits, luring dancers from the stage. But tradition is subverted, by breaking her visual field into millions of possibilities. What is occurring in the wings has no more substance than what is happening on stage. The same process applies to the performer's whole body: her seeing subverts purpose. Thus, while maintaining the logic of a forward-moving path, there is a substantial redivision of choices being noticed in and outside her body.

I have many fittings with my costumer Susan Norwood. She crochets a midnight blue skullcap, laced with gold and cobalt thread and tiny beads. She dyes a silk dress the same blue blackness. Its sheer bodice fits snugly over a cobalt unitard. Quasi-stiff organza forms loosely fitted long sleeves that end in a vee at the base of each pinkie. A modest v-neckline at the front and back of the bodice is edged with a single line of gold stitching.

The lower part of the dress is silk shantung. An inverted vee peaks at the base of the sternum. Its two sides slope, curving around to the spine, meeting at the waistline. The skirt gradually spreads out from the body, maintaining an oval shape built into the dress with three tiers of progressively wider wire supports, twenty-six inches wide at the lowest ring. A line of gold stitching inconspicuously highlights the inverted v-line and the three oval rings.

My daughter's shoes are in a plastic shopping bag tucked behind a chair near the front door in my living room the morning she leaves home to seek fame and fortune in Los Angeles. A few days later, I phone to ask about the shoes. "Take them to Goodwill or keep them," she says. Her feet are smaller than mine, yet the shoes fit and complete the costume for *Exit*.

From the base of the skirt, my cobalt-stockinged feet fit into Savannah's black suede maryjanes. I want her to notice that her shoes travel one path yet the dancer in them steers free of a single destination.

Each time the dancer turns to look back, she feels an overbearing recall of personal history steeped in heartbreak, and loss. When the last turn is made, instead of contemplating the past, the dancer keeps turning, passing through the past back into the present. She disengages from the past, but it is not erased. In a moment's absorption the past is recognized and carried forward—past and future, exiting and entering, direct yet without linearity, wound and suspended. The stage empties with the dancer's entrance into its wings.

Exit, 1995. Photo © 1997 by Emma Hanson.

15　my body equates patience with renewal

> Playing is the mask of nothing at all.
> —*Thomas Whitaker,* teacher

More than a year of work-related commitments would have me on tour from May 1996 through September 1997. I was playing whatever cards I could to ensure financial stability, and thus my attention was drawn to opportunities outside of Austin, the city where I live.

Like other experimental artists, I am learning to redefine home. My city, state, and country are not predisposed to treat me as theirs. In the arts columns, in their minds, or on the streets, perhaps. At the box office, no dice. The compulsion to expose, renegotiate, or reinvent the strengths and weaknesses of dance tradition offers little in its final outcome to attract the average dance-goer.

The tour was to begin in Montreal in late May 1996 and end sixteen months later in California. I had to find a way not to burn out. To prepare, I would arbitrarily pause during the day and (not unlike opening a medicine kit and removing a syringe), would inject myself with the phrase *my body equates patience with renewal.* My body chemistry immediately altered. Space parted my lungs, thoughts I did not know I was thinking would cease, my breath rose, and an inner calm would spread like sudden mist.

July 1996, on a tiny island in East Long Pond, Vermont, no cabins or people were in sight. I came in a red canoe, a little afraid because the wind was up. Nervousness followed me as I climbed the island's single wooded hill where my bare feet sank into the underbrush and my footing became unsure. As small as the island was, I worried about finding the canoe later. I had paddled to the island in search of a message, a piece of the big puzzle. Discomfort prevailed. I injected *my*

East Long Pond, Vermont. Photo by Deborah Hay.

body equates patience with renewal and the dosage ended my seeking. I relaxed on a mossy hillock, overlooking grasses where a loon sat nesting. I found a certain amount of humor in witnessing the effectiveness of this medicine.

By the time I left for New Zealand at the end of August 1996, and for the next year, my metaphorical home was regularly boosted with the help of my imaginary medicine bag. I danced, taught, performed, was an artist-in-residence, and I wrote at other people's desks. I was accommodated beautifully among wonderful people for many weeks at a time. I turned fifty-five in Amsterdam and received a pair of red crystal floweret earrings from my students. *My body equates patience with renewal* provided a home for me.

An East Indian doctor of acupuncture, nutrition, osteopathy, and naturopathy asked me about fear. My symptoms implied its presence. "I worry about supporting myself as I get older," I told him. He responded, "You are a successful artist. Why do you create fear?" I repeated my concerns and elaborated about the struggle of many artists in this country, particularly at this time. But he was no longer listening.

Years ago, I gave a dinner party for a group of women friends in Austin. I wanted them to meet Carolee Schneemann, who had just arrived to teach in the art department at the University of Texas. Days before the party, I completed twenty-two nights of performances in a room that had been converted into a studio at the back of my house. Around the table after dinner, I mentioned to the women that I was feeling low and out-of-sorts. Carolee responded: "You have just performed every night for three weeks and your community is without a tradition for honoring you." Without pause, my tears began running.

My sense of home has changed in other ways, including how I work. I conducted an annual four-month workshop for trained and untrained dancers in Austin, Texas, from 1980 through 1996. In January, when Playing Awake 1996 began, I knew that it would be the last, although I tried to make it appear otherwise. Deep in my heart, I knew that what I teach had never been more clear to me. But misery bloomed when we barely had thirteen participants and those included trades, partial and full scholarships, and others begging in with installment plans. Financially, it was a cut and paste job, but how could I tell students who had arrived from Europe, New York, and Washington state to turn around and go home? This was not the first workshop to fail financially, but I kept thinking it was a fluke. It took me time to acknowledge three prior flukes. In practical terms the demise of Playing Awake brought an end to my attempt to form a financial safety net.

I wasn't getting what I needed from the workshops anymore, on more fronts than financial. I was trying to keep something alive that had outlived its creative purpose. What had been for so many years an inspirational laboratory for artistic growth and expansion, for the spirit it aroused in me and the others, for reading the dance in everyone, each moment, equally, no matter what anyone was doing, had run its course.

My interest has narrowed. I want to work with experienced performers who are interested in exploring the more subtle boundaries of visible performance consciousness, work which, understandably, has limited interest for untrained performers. I want to choreograph exacting movement content that contains no end to discovery, where milliseconds of stunning recognition take place within a strict choreography in time and space. Where soundless rhythms drive the dance.

I remove the medicine kit, inject another dose, and my lungs get the attention the doctor ordered.

16 my body hears many voices, not one voice

> The key to multi-level existence is deep listening. Deep
> listening includes all sound as well as language and its syntax,
> the nature of its sound, atmosphere, and environmental
> context. This is essential to the process of unlocking layer after
> layer of imagination, meaning, and memory, down to the
> cellular level of human experience. Listening is the key to
> performance. Responses—whatever the discipline—that
> originate from deep listening are connected in resonance with
> being and inform the artist, art, and audience in an effortless
> harmony.
> —*Pauline Oliveros*, composer

 OR, THE TOWER OF BABEL REVISITED

for seven performers
April 1993, Austin, Texas
choreography Deborah Hay

CHOREOGRAPHER'S NOTE: Some of the movement descriptions may seem incomplete. It is because at times my capacity to differentiate between one movement, mine for example, as being more appropriate in the moment than one of the dancer's seems unreasonable. Rather, if I am in the position of not knowing how a dancer will manifest a set of movement directions, my interest as well as the dancer's is consistently heightened, especially when one is observing or applying oneself to several months of practice. This choreographic incompleteness could be considered an immersion into a larger sense of choreography. Here the performer exercises a practiced trust in the cellular body's momentary configuration. Adjectives like unexplainable, unidentifiable, tricky, formless, ancient rites, unpatterned, suggest the dark side of performance life—the un-named, unknown, unforeseen half. To indicate where this material occurs in the score, the symbol ⊙ will appear in the margin.

The spoken text was re-created as I was typing the dance score. In fact, for four months the individual performers practiced spontaneously invented speech, deliberately excluding any accent that might suggest an already existing language.

LIST OF PERFORMERS (*character descriptions were assigned in the weeks following the dance performance, after seeing the video, and while I was writing the movement score*):

Michael Arnold: **skirt-man**—a calf-length, a-line skirt accentuated skirt-man's shoulders. His outstanding feature is an electric-like charge that radiates through his physical bearing.

Beverly Bajema: **bare-headed one**—a devoted practitioner who periodically shaves her head. She reflects clarity and experience.

Jewell Handy: **american african american**—part of Jewell's identification of herself the first day of the workshop. This does not limit her other identities.

Meg McHutchison: **woman-in-a-slip**—a tall, mid-western body in a sexy undergarment. Characteristically intellectual, statuesque, and earnest.

Grace Mi-He Lee: **asian woman**—a young, Korean-American dancer. She sneezes, laughs, and tells jokes, dancing. She is sharp and committed.

Jason Phelps: **young actor**—obvious to the viewer. He is gangly, focused, and theatrical.

Ginger Rhodes Cain: **witch**—a mother and artist, with long brown hair and recurring quizzical expressions. She possesses farm girl elegance.

They are costumed in varying shades of ordinary black clothing.

PRESET:
The lobby walls exhibit written and graphic responses to a public request for personal interpretations of ⊙ , the symbol used to identify this dance event.

Calling cards with the symbol and request had been issued to the community weeks earlier.

Tower sculptures stand in the studio lobby. They are made by Beverly Bajema, Austin artist Ken Burns, and students from Linda Montano's performance art class at the University of Texas.

For two mornings prior to the event the choreographer and performers scrub scuff marks from the floor in the studio/theater.

Eight risers hold five folding chairs apiece. They are separated from one another like islands. Newspaper is spread, covering the floor of each platform. Beverly Bajema finds foreign press to arrange along the front border of each riser.

Pressed white bed sheets are individually suspended from rods that lift them just off the floor. They hang at slightly different angles and collectively cover the upstage wall and create two pairs of wings on either side of the stage area. Seven hats and canes are indiscriminately spread across the upstage floor, unnoticeable to the audience.

In the candlelit hallway leading into the studio, six brass candlesticks stand on a piano top that is draped in sheer white cotton. The angle of the piano guides the audience through a doorway into the performing area. The choreographer dances in an unlit hallway beyond the piano. It is not her intention to attract the audience as they pass into the theater, but she imagines she can influence the subconscious activity about to occur there. She understands just how audacious, ludicrous, and practicable this is.

A soft white glow permeates the studio. After the audience is seated, the light fades to black, enveloping the audience in total darkness for a brief period.

Woman-in-a-slip, asian woman, witch, and bare-headed one enter the darkness and go to prescribed places upstage. They lie flat on their backs with their heads in a straight line paralleling the audience. Their feet rest directly upstage nearly touching the "curtains."

LIGHT SLOWLY RISES.

The following five separate simultaneous changes take about six and a half minutes to perform. The timing between the changes is deliberately unpredictable. Each change, performed with absolute economy, arises from and completes itself in stillness.

Four women lie with their backs on the floor for a long time.

CHANGE 1: As if slipped through a crack in time, four pairs of legs are in the air, slightly spread and perpendicular to the floor. Four pairs of arms and hands stretch vertically in the space between the vee of the opened legs.

CHANGE 2: Four women spring to sitting with their backs to us, legs crossed yoga-style in front of them. After a short pause each dancer gets busy with similar unidentifiable movement activity. The clothing in some instances obscures the movement, but their personal intent is visibly cohesive and pure. Four sets of barefoot toes appear under each woman's hips. It is quiet. Straight backs and silent bearings.

CHANGE 3: Simultaneously, four heads turn to look over four left shoulders. So, too, the arms, to the left of the torso, are curved upward, u-shaped, with architectural certainty. Furthest left, woman-in-a-slip's arms are above her shoulders. Each woman in turn holds her arms slightly lower so that bare-headed one, furthest right, curves hers opposite her hips. Although heads face arms, the gaze is not riveted there. The performers are practicing a more inclusive seeing — through, around, and beyond their arms.

CHANGE 4: Each set of hands returns to its lap as each head realigns with the straight spine. *Some days, if I blink, I miss the changes.* The women are consistently poised.

CHANGE 5: The heads turn to the right as the curved arms reappear on the right side of the body. This time the arms appear softer, more feminine.

After a period of stillness, the four women begin to rise from the floor, without a particular form. As they ascend, the american african american woman enters from the audience and runs upstage, on the balls of her feet, taking uncomfortably small steps, at once quick and tentative. The light-skinned soles of her feet peek out at us. She leans slightly in the direction she is stepping, always facing away from us. The other four women are stopped mid-action, two facing diagonally upstage left and two right.

Nearly flush with them, american african american woman pauses before slowly pivoting to the audience, a commanding presence directed at us. One palm is stretched open facing her heart and the other is inches from her belly. She is babbling yet her deep voice sounds wildly familiar to the ear.

american african american: Unterrat sher poin letundrateet
raggoltoit. Frabolettaring urdoot pobblerack spot. Iper
iperdorabb hounsunleter.

Turning away, she gradually diminishes the volume and intensity of her words. She throws her head back, arching the top of her spine before descending like a ship to the bottom of the ocean. Like a continent on the move she haltingly crawls backward to the furthest downstage corner. Rising quickly, she spins continuously, swinging the weight of her head in front and behind to topple her balance. It seems she will run into the women as she rushes toward them spinning. Abruptly stopping, she cries, "sock . . . ," as if calling to a sister. She listens to her voice ricochet. The audience has no idea she said "sock."

Hearing "sock," the four women turn to face the audience, using a variety of unexplainable arm movements to augment the turn. They are now in a straight line across the back of the stage, one spread palm hovering at the heart and the other opposite the belly.

The american african american woman throws herself into three full-throttled leaps, pausing precariously between each one. Arriving upstage, two women flank her on either side as she performs faux-tribal rites. In unison the four women pull themselves forward behind her, using the magnetism in their hands to draw their vertical bodies forward. They are capable of taking only one tiny step at a time. Their orderliness is a disturbingly humorous adjunct to her exoticism.

Two men enter from each side of the audience, dancing. One carries a hat and one a cane. Their movements suggest a soft-shoe. Sidling up beside the american african american, she is handed the cane. The hat is placed in her other hand. The moment the hat is accepted, the four women, behind the trio, swing both u-shaped arms out to the right, looking over the right shoulder as the hips shift left. In unison they switch and shift from side to side arhythmically.

The trio performs a barely suggested hat-and-cane routine. Once in a while a sudden jerk rocks the american african american, but she returns to the dreamy soft-shoe. Several spasms later, she peremptorily returns the hat to one gentleman and cane to the other. The men freeze when the objects are placed in their hands. Approaching the audience with forward-moving, lurching steps, she babbles in reverse.

american african american: IIchillebraetta schmootteratt einto
    rabulluoptraichor. Hebbit firryout iimm. Harbbutop uprellot.
    Kroit munglerep.

She spins around to face the others. They instantly respond by filling the stage with large shattering movements.

LIGHT FADES *on this frenetic field of activity.*
BLACKOUT.

LIGHT SLOWLY RETURNS, *exposing the performers in quietly composed activity.*

Everyone except asian woman is scootching forward in tiny little increments, with arms pressed into their tightly held bodies. They are wriggling, not unlike vertically oriented snakes, to a prescribed place in a semicircle facing away from center stage. Each dancer steps out of the wriggle into a visibly hesitant position. Bare-headed one, unbelievably thorough in her performance practice, is usually last to arrive because her tiny little steps do not waver. In the following order from stage right to left are: bare-headed one, witch, skirt-man, woman-in-a-slip, american african american, young actor.

Asian woman is half her height, on her knees, her arms at her sides facing upstage. It looks as though mild shocks of electricity randomly shoot through her. Being on her knees gives the movement a swiveling effect. Individual members of the group intermittently turn toward her with the heel of the hand placed under the chin, fingers stretched toward her. Babble is briefly produced before they twist back to a hesitant stance.

bare-headed one: Roibllet hundrwentermont heddle. Krequop krep it letterat voul.

skirt-man: Sekki! harvop ittlemanb hrew. Lemeant zup. Trekkel gronmit.

witch: Plunmb. Hubvrew. Axtimopill culter. Hadrenc vow tuttellonderboig.

Etc.

Asian woman spirals up from the floor facing us, a palm stretched over her heart and one at her belly. The dance she performs is unrepentingly bizarre. It is as if she is obeying the rules of a diabolical scientist. As her face slides and falls, her body responds. Her arms drop, she jumps down onto the balls of her feet and stops, spine rigid. As if fixed, she performs two fast, tiny, efficient jumps and then she stops. Three jumps, stop. Four, stop. Five, stop. Six, stop. During seven she drops on her butt and in the shape of a saucer locomotes backward with legs in the air and arms waving. She pulls herself halfway to standing before falling back to the saucer-shaped locomotion, legs and arms waving. She repeats this a number of times before getting to her feet. Knees slightly bowed, she runs backward, occasionally using her upper arm to pull herself backward around herself. Wherever she lands after the spin determines the direction she resumes running. She runs backward again and again before emerging from the frenzy to tentatively call out "sock. . . ." At that moment the cast turns to her, chin supported by the heel of the hand, and in unison they babble:

bare-headed one: Undeel poi. Hartovrew hundattersly. Grepoin croilt herberattemcroil rubbergleck treckop. Quoi reedwop cixvil youickkl.

witch: lf trodderlen plet. Poijeracklerek grembrot. Serloc verloc hemlock hordett trw. Quontopredullproec hexcratellof poingerage. Dond. Donterfreb.

skirt-man: Trennder hoop loorwegglebrat. Hybregredisnso.Rectrzanderwork. Donhvrem lenkerpoltice. He. Terwinklebot bot leb tres. Poiltrolixterettleno.

woman-in-a-slip: Jel. Oplriggerrot manecknerbarb. Kriste lupenob. Ikremvrel. Ply torreck. Rennw itt haprenoppelgrin. Plegeratingord sleinken.

american african american: Grellinpret boil. Kelliomunberattle rull quot dup. Foingy crewquot. Vrenyfail biedix hopletreg. Gre! Gretem! Gretemplo.

young actor: Ooile frebremcret partipery inklot. Keew kraw trat. Zelle wekee treop. Wellendixterhandle hoplert yangf. Rex harpittle tureenvaximperilt.

Asian woman neurologically responds to the onslaught of babble. She walks diagonally downstage right as if she is on a spring hillside with grasses blowing. She evokes a shepherdess with her flock as the others follow crawling backward on their hands and knees.

asian woman: Loiid predder heek.

They rise and as a tribe cross the front edge of the stage at a moderate pace. Each performs a unique sequence of movements, not too much or too little. No one person or movement is distinguishable. On the way we hear

asian woman: Enkleeart nooikled wenk.

Further on:

asian woman: Oik, derbiot.

When the last dancer passes center stage, the group simultaneously begins traveling backward, retracing the path until the new last dancer recrosses center stage. Still the unique sequence of movements, not too much or too little, no one person or movement distinguishable, is being danced.

Everyone in unison does an about-face, recrossing the stage again but traveling backward to the door that was left open after the audience entered the studio. When it is reached, in unison, they do a second about-face and stay caught, mid-action, framed in the doorway.

Asian woman leaves the group to advance onto the empty stage, going about this way and that, undoing continuity of movement except for glimpses of hat-and-cane dancing. She shakes recurrent aggressive movements from her body before turning away. With grand implications streaming from her back she highlights her passage upstage with very very short, powerful, screams.

asian woman: AAAE!

asian woman: AEAE!

asian woman: EAEA!

When the screams end, the cast turns in unison to proceed unsurely upstage except for skirt-man. (While the group is still in the doorway, he leaves stage to slip on a mid-length, black, flared skirt over his biking shorts.) He sidles onstage, his back to us. His body draws itself up onto its toes again and again, like liquid through a straw.

Skirt-man looks menacing. His back is immobile though we hear him breathing. He looks as if he will blow apart. The others' bodies, upstage from him, reflect tension and admonition as they walk.

He takes off in fistfuls of fanning movements that disrupt the vertical continuity of the group. They spread from his immediate range. Physical well-being at stake, they check to see where he is before resuming their own actions. For much of the remainder of skirt-man's solo the other performers stay grouped stage left using a variety of rapid, spatially reduced, unexplainable arm movements to augment each turn to or away from the audience. All, when facing the audience, have one palm spread opposite the heart and the other opposite the belly; their faces are in flux.

Skirt-man's large, unpredictably aggressive movement leads him upstage. Almost on the tips of his toes, his palm is spread open at his heart, the other flattened at his solar plexus. Sauntering toward us, holding his energy tightly across his chest, he inhales and exhales loudly. His eyeglasses sporadically flash light from the right or left lens. He returns to the group and disturbs their efforts to cohere. He passes through them with bullying magnetism. He leaps hammer-like, spins, throws himself into and away from them, and recedes to the upstage right corner of the stage. He collapses on one knee with both hands on the floor in front of him, head down.

The group meanwhile has formed a straight line paralleling the audience. In unison, they swing their tightly curved u-shaped arms to one side of their bodies or the other; together they can start or stop a chorus of staccato barking sounds, without acting like dogs. Skirt-man rises spinning across stage, his skirt flaring around his knees, and once more disturbs the order of the group by heading straight into it. His hands rise to his ears. On half-toe he looks for woman-in-a-slip. Finding her, he takes her hand in his. She stops her fake bark and the two of them make their way to center stage not knowing how to dance together. The group stops barking and begins to mimic stillness.

LIGHT FADES *on the duet not knowing how to dance together.*

The cast re-positions itself.

LIGHT RETURNS.

Woman-in-a-slip is facing upstage seated Japanese-style. Clustered directly to her left, the others watch her intently throughout her dance. She looks at them, looks down, looks back, and then raises her arms toward them. With care, she slides her arms around to the front of her body. She could be holding a camera. A second version of this arm movement, more like a mother rocking a child, is performed to her right, away from the group. A sense of awkward intimacy including wide hands and beautifully articulated fingers looking for a place to be, carries her to her feet. She whispers intermittently, turning around herself, circling the group. She does not know how to direct her intimacy. The captivated group follows her with its gaze. An intimate remark, delivered in the time it takes to say "take off your clothes," may be directed at her from anyone in the group.

bare-headed woman: Eech lat sud rat.

skirt-man: Wieru fotm ggot mltkop.

young actor: Jhn ve mokn jiy.

Etc.

Woman-in-a-slip finishes circling, then presses the front of her body onto the floor, tucking her hands under her belly. She twists and pulls herself to her knees and then stands. She could be performing a strip, a sex act, or making love, except the gestures do not match. Spread wide, she boldly faces her audience. One stretched palm is pulled onto her stomach and the other is placed high against her chest. Removing the hand from the chest, she places its heel onto the underside of her chin and presses her head backward into an arch involving her entire spine. All remain intimately connected to her. Making one more circle, this time away from the group, woman-in-a-slip reaches the furthest point from them, when witch steps forward and in her own quirky, charismatic, flippant way, dances. Woman-in-a-slip slips into the group before witch reaches center stage.

LIGHT FADES *on dainty boldness in the form of a dancing witch character.*

LIGHT RETURNS.

We see the wriggling, vertical, snake-like locomotive dance; the cast, minus the witch, finding its prescribed location in a large semicircle filling the stage. Each performer assumes a puffed-up, superhuman posture in celebration of the witch.

Witch faces upstage with both arms curved in a u-shape to her right. She captures us with her stillness before making a quixotic passage to stage left. Pressing into the wall with her hands, she bows her spine, drops her head, springs off the wall, and crosses the stage, a fast-forward cinematic image without a sure reference. She sees each dancer along her route.

Reaching bare-headed one at the farthest end of the semicircle, she carefully steps behind her, attaching her own spine, as if magnetically, to bare-headed one's.

Disengaging, she takes time to choose exactly where to step, selecting the direction to place her foot before drawing the arch of the other foot to the heel of the first. In this manner, she methodically follows the semicircle, visiting each performer. Her body is regally aligned. With animal patience, she respectively encounters bare-headed one, asian woman, skirt-man, and woman-in-a-slip. Each one in turn responds with a shrill, high-pitched volley of speech:

bare-headed one: Itsta lurnt weethartyangit. Ifffy weandgrt. Loit, loit . . . , etc.

asian woman: Feeklanders rote. Omintullilliott remandcrad. Hoid illiioter wageeeter . . . , etc.

skirt-man: Fummertrac wadd tippertnub. Hoblliett rotta weftrek lok . . . , etc.

woman-in-a-slip: Boiblemilitre itst remmectrac quiquiqui. Voil . . . , etc.

Each voice joins the next as witch passes their pompous stances. When she arrives at woman-in-a-slip, the four she has passed simultaneously step toward and behind witch woman, inflated poses intact, traveling in such a way as not to disturb the posture imposed on the top half of their bodies. Their high-pitched voices gradually diminish in volume. As witch woman passes american african american all shapes drop and with baby steps they all follow the steady witch offstage. Only the young actor does not exit. One palm opened at his heart, the other opposite his belly, he is awash in small changes.

The others return, retracing their recent exit, walking backward. As they pass behind the young actor, he erupts in darts, spins, pivots, falls; he is a needle, spun into a whirlwind of tricky floor patterns that stretch everyone's capacity to follow. The group works to stay directly behind him, suggesting his flurry in their bodies, but his movement defies space and time. He never seems anywhere long enough. He makes a screeching stop, the heel of his hand beneath the tip of his chin. The group, breathless and still, stands behind him anticipating his next move. The young actor performs a spare hat-and-cane dance without a hat or cane. The others join in, independently arriving midstage, creating a horizontal line facing us. One at a time, each one drops out of the soft-shoe into familial stillness. Light remains on everyone captured in a line of moments.

LIGHTS OUT. *In darkness the performers try to locate their real hats and canes spread randomly and inconspicuously in a line across the upstage floor.*

LIGHTS UP.

We see a hodge-podge of performers looking for their hats and canes, readying them on their bodies, or beginning the next section of the dance. A multitude of insinuating hat-and-cane-like dance movements brings them toward us. The young actor and skirt-man fake stillness halfway downstage. In a line directly in front of us, the women continue a hat-and-cane charade. Who they are is never certain. Appearances come and go. They add an occasional, short, aggressive whip of the body that topples the hat and the object being used as a cane, i.e., an umbrella, string, stick, staff.

Skirt-man straightens up, leaving the young actor and the stage.

With arms outspread, the women slowly retreat upstage emitting sporadic fractions-of-a-yell.

american african american woman: AA-

bare-headed one: WHE-

asian woman: EE-

Left to right, seated: Grace Mi-He Lee, Beverly Bajema, Ginger Rhodes Cain; standing: Jason Phelps, Meg McHutchison, Mike Arnold, Jewell Handy. Photo © 1993 by Phyllis Liedeker.

witch: YA

woman-in-a-slip: IE- . . . AR-

Once upstage, the physically expanded women stay still.

Meanwhile the young actor is bent and frozen. Nothing happens until skirt-man struts back to stage, casually aligning himself with the young actor, mimicking his physical posture as closely as possible. They enter a discussion that seems to be about the correct placement of their bodies but soon covers other topics that we cannot be sure of. They change from posture to posture, one assuming the stance of the other. Mostly they discuss things.

skirt-man: Rigletersticunp it provoolprepict harragul. Ned?

young actor: Roqur tnun bnatpnunpisthbottung, thih loo hojt fifbromf hoh nax, len henhoj honbonxipriwi lokhajttalhieo, usaojifpseoigemd, nit sajyikirrpoh klahamrest.

skirt-man: Asad fovembinrisut. Hotnaviz nicropiyn un merhekt ritron uomet iumeoitrepo, minrup mabnuyo yeertyu tiy utyut roty rityr.

young actor: Nottubnitndemegn. Plo rigjen em. Asjzex denkeknemnnenr, nibi, harteii.

skirt-man: Yetnunbodmiv! It, hahsosf hajow.

Without warning, skirt-man and young actor flip and shatter space with frenetic and unpredictable dancing. Their action throws the five women into similar chaos.

LIGHT FADES.

LIGHT RETURNS.

Six of the seven performers walk into the audience and exit leaving bare-headed one alone onstage.

It is difficult to describe her actions. It doesn't seem to be necessary.

bare-headed one: "ppnk"

Her dance is punctuated with a sound that may be a word or not.

bare-headed one: "pnkk"

It is not like watching a human being.

bare-headed one: "pnnk."

SLOW FADE *to darkness.*

17 my body relaxes when thoughts abate

> Thoughts are filters that get clogged by history, habits and ambitions, blocking the flow of uncharted responses to unmeasured now.
> —Robert Rauschenberg, artist

3 DANCES

O

Say *O*
O—O—O...
an old o
before there was a letter

Say *you*
you—you—you...
before there was a me

Say *me*
me—me...
before there was there

Lament

first phrase:
ahhh bow (like the bow before arrow)
same note same duration

second phrase:
ahhh bow dahh day
bow, a flatted second higher than *a h h h*.
d a h h, a flatted third higher than *a h h h*.
day, same note as *b o w*
all notes are equal
the two phrases repeatable

meanwhile:
the ball of the feet
slap upon stone
tap steps counter
the four-note drone.

Opening

Show five fingers or ten.
Say "four," then "or,"
Look around
"or"
"more." Yes!
"Roar." Speak it.
"Boom."
"Roar."

"Wait!"
"Come," good humoredly.
"Come," you urge.
Say "crack place inside"
I think blood flows backward
everything returns to nothing.

The three dances are dedicated to Cynthia Jean Cohen Bull who died September 27, 1996. Cynthia Jean Cohen Bull was a dancer, choreographer, anthropologist, researcher, teacher, and producer. She practiced an uninterrupted, open-minded inquiry into all types of dancing. With her husband, Richard Bull, they created the Warren Street Performance Loft in New York City, where I often performed my solo work. Clear, abrupt laughter is how I remember Cynthia most. Richard followed her lead into death. Their absence and their presence are irreplaceable.

18 my body is held in the present
or, attending a dance performance in 2097

> From the floor, I picked up what I thought was a seed. As it
> came to life in my hand, my thumb rolled it across my fingers
> and dropped it. The spider ran. My hand still knows that supple
> spider body.
> —Simone Forti, dancer

There are no tickets or reserved seats. I don't know where the dance
performance is and I am not to look for nor anticipate the location.
The choreographer whose work I am about to see suggests that the
small group consisting of her audience/patrons apply her frame of
reference for seeing dance before we leave home.

In the humming quarters of a grooming tank, I am bathed, moistur-
ized, and massaged. My clothes contain stimulants that heighten the
sensitivity of my skin.

I leave for the performance without locking the door. It seals itself
shut when it senses my body crossing the threshold. Keys long ago
replaced arrowheads as objects of the hunt for the hobbyist collector.

After centuries of disregard, particularly in cities, the moon, stars,
and fire have again become the primary source of evening light. Un-
encumbered boulevards are bordered with vegetable, flower, and
herb gardens, and orchards tended and harvested by their respective
communities. Tangy scents open my temples and nasal passages, and
my salivary glands juice excitedly. Everything radiates, and my surface
capillaries blissfully respond.

Humans *have* learned to see life as scintillating composites of every
conceivable combination of matter that has ever been, is, or will be.
Through disciplined practice and guidance from early childhood, we

have unlearned the compulsion to judge life by a mere handful of facts. Our cultural commitment to embrace the unknown, particularly after the demise of the computer age, reminds me to breathe deeply and notice everything.

The choreographer had one other suggestion. "Turn in place several times and then walk in the direction you face when you stop turning." And so I do, glad to be going where I haven't chosen to be. The act and object of seeing are now undifferentiated. I am the performance I set out to find without looking, alert to fleeting changes in and outside my physical body. Breathing feels planetary. My hands pass and turn like tropical vegetation before my eyes.

People enter my visual field. We are interacting no matter what we do. Like that man sitting with his head lowered and his eyes closed. On one level, he does not register my presence. On another, we are including each other in our separate perceptions of the moment. I love this feeling. I love him for being where he is so I can see him in this context.

A blind woman with ivory-colored skin and a downy layer of body hair moves along the street in tiny little steps. She is wearing a black bathing suit. Her legs glide over the surface of the boulevard. She is completely at ease, a smile turning her half-opened eyes into slits. Her guide, a young woman with fine black eyes and an aquiline nose, watches the blind woman from a distance, her patience and goodwill palpable. If the motion of the blind woman looks threatened by outside interference, her guide is immediately beside her to prevent harm. She moves so rapidly her work is invisible.

A tall, broad-shouldered woman wearing an ankle-length cobalt blue skirt holds an edge of the skirt at arm's length. Her head is tilted downward and she focuses several feet beyond her body. With the skirt edge in her hand, she thoughtfully steps forward on one leg, the other coming to meet it like an old friend. The poetry of being so close to stillness is hypnotic. She, too, has another person aligned with her. It is difficult to tell if this person is male or female. The body is small, fit, and fast-moving like a hawk. It swoops into place to ground the tall, blue-skirted woman. Blue skirt moves. Hawk flashes into her field and becomes perfectly still. Blue skirt moves away. Hawk stays. It is impossible to read meaning into this strange dynamic.

An infectious joy exudes from a tall, thin, good-looking man who gallops by, wearing a red cape and clown's nose. His teeth are bared.

In a bed of flowers, a woman stands with her hands spreading and resting on the voluptuous surfaces of her body. She is large-breasted, with a rounded belly and big eyes. The pleasure she experiences is doubly appreciated in the absence of any embarrassment. Near her, a dark-featured man sits in a lotus position barking like a dog. People flinch at the sound but return to what they were doing, more alert and laughing.

A gypsy family passes in a loose file. There are nine of them, their manner quiet and easy. Straight backs, heads high, their dark eyes flash and their hair falls casually. They disappear through a doorway framed by green leaves. My eyes roam in the empty frame.

A parade appears at the end of the boulevard. Pairs of nervous black horses draw carriages with young children dressed in stiff lace clothing; or they pull floats engorged with color and beauty. Other boys and girls watch from tents lining the parade route. Wide-eyed and ecstatic, their chins rest on the backs of their hands, which are folded atop railings separating them from the passing river of music, color, and stunning happiness. I am reminded of a culture once known as Mexican.

A woman standing alone is trying to determine how to prepare a few potatoes that lie nested in her apron. She thinks about it for a long time. At her side, a gray-haired woman tells a tale of life, love, and death, spoken so quietly I must burrow down to hear.

An old woman with foreshortened arms jumps to clutch the branch of a tree. The sound is *suck*. She tells jokes with her body; about a four-legged fish and a two-legged fish; then fish.

A dark-brown-skinned musician stands in ankle-deep water playing jazz on a primitive stringed instument. His feet pad the silt of the river bottom, as he pulls sand up over one foot with the other. The water does not cloud. Another man enters this river that is more green than blue. Beside him a baby is born, curling into a fetal position before I get a chance to see it. One set of identical twins hands the newborn to another set of identical twins. Everyone is pleased. I glance at the time. It is 11:33.

I love this choreographer.

a chronicle of performance practices by Deborah Hay

1970–80: I imagine every cell in my body hears, performs, and surrenders the dance simultaneously.

1980–85: The whole body at once is the teacher.

1985: I imagine every cell in my body invites being seen perceiving no movement wrong, out of place, or out of character.

1986: I invite being seen whole and changing. You remind me of my wholeness changing.

1987: I imagine every cell in my body has the potential to perceive wisdom every moment, while remaining positionless about what wisdom is or what it looks like.

1988: I imagine every cell in my body has the potential to perceive movement as nourishment which supports movement which is nourishment, etc. etc.

1989: I imagine every cell in my body at once invites being seen not being fixed in my fabulously unique three-dimensional body. I imagine every cell in my body perceives the three-dimensional body as a sleight of hand.

1990: I imagine every cell in my body perceives that alignment is everywhere.

1991: Every cell in my body invites being seen just so.

1991–92: Every cell in my body invites being seen living and dying at once. Wherever I am dying is. What if dying is movement in communion with all there is? What if impermanence is a steadily transforming present? Seeing impermanence requires admitting that nothing I see is forever. I am the impermanence I see.

1992: I imagine every cell in my body has the potential to perceive ah-ha! and nada (nothing), at once.

1993–94: What if tower is a metaphor for consciousness and babble is the reality check? Tower is the attention. Babble is each moment of movement. I imagine every cell in my body at once has the

potential to perceive the toweringness of its babble; the
perfection of chaos, a constantly shattering, nondiminishing
tower.

1995: I imagine my whole body at once has the potential to dialogue
with all there is.

1995 –96: What if where I am is what I need? Wherever I am is what
I need. Everywhere I am is what I need.

1996: What if my whole body at once has the potential to perceive
Here, spatially, including everything I see and everything I can't
see, now, and now, and now? What if Now is my past, present,
and future here, here, and here?

1997–98: What if now is here is harmony?

1999: What if every cell in my body at once had the potential to
locate and choose the oxygen it needs to keep my fire burning?

DEBORAH HAY is "an experimentalist in soul and body" (*New York Times*) and "a phenomenon capable of expanding and diversifying the language of movement in the most striking and unexpected ways" (*Dance Australia*). Her choreography, from exquisitely meditative solos to dances for large groups of untrained and trained dancers, explores the nature of experience, perception, and attention in dance. Hay has received numerous awards and fellowships in recognition of her groundbreaking choreography Her previous books are *Moving Through the Universe in Bare Feet* (1975) and *Lamb at the Altar: The Story of a Dance* (1994).

In 1960, at the age of nineteen, Deborah Hay moved from Brooklyn into Manhattan. Her choreographic work developed in the midst of the most radical cultural revolution in the United States. Hay was one of the early members of the Judson Dance Theatre, a community of artists whose work challenged the foundational principles of modern dance, from who dances to the very notion of what constitutes a dance. In 1964 she toured with the Merce Cunningham Dance Company. By 1967 she was choreographing exclusively for untrained dancers. Hay left New York in 1970 to live in a community in northern Vermont. It was here that she began to follow a rigorous daily performance practice which continues to inform her as a student, teacher, and dancer. In 1976 she moved with her daughter, Savannah, to Austin, Texas, and began performing as a solo artist for the first time. From 1980 through 1996 she conducted fifteen annual large group workshops. These group dances became the fabric for her solo performance repertory. Hay has become a prominent figure in both the local and the international dance community, where she is praised not only for her performances but also as an extraordinary teacher and advocate.

SUSAN FOSTER is Professor of Dance History at University of California–Riverside and the author of *Choreography and Narrative: Ballet's Staging of Story and Desire* (Indiana University Press, 1998) and *Reading Dancing: Bodies and Subjects in Contemporary American Dance* (University of California Press, 1988). She is the editor of *Choreographing History* (Indiana University Press, 1995) and *Corporealities: Dancing Knowledge, Culture and Power* (Routledge, 1995).